OHIO
DOMINICAN
UNIVERSITY™

SINCE 1911

CHINA'S SON

CHINA'S SON

Growing Up in the Cultural Revolution

Da Chen

Delacorte Press

Published by
Delacorte Press
an imprint of
Random House Children's Books
a division of Random House, Inc.
1540 Broadway
New York, New York 10036

Visit us on the Web! www.randomhouse.com/teens
Educators and librarians, for a variety of teaching tools,
visit us at www.randomhouse.com/teachers

Library of Congress Cataloging-in-Publication Data

Chen, Da.
    China's son : growing up in the Cultural Revolution / Da Chen.
        p. cm.
    ISBN 0-385-72929-4
        1. Chen, Da, 1962—Juvenile literature. 2. China—Biography—Juvenile literature.
3. China—History—Cultural Revolution, 1966–1976—Personal narratives—Juvenile
literature. [1. Chen, Da, 1962– 2. China—Biography. 3. China—History—Cultural
Revolution, 1966–1976—Personal narratives.] I. Title: Growing up in the Cultural
Revolution. II. Title.

CT1828.C5214 A3 2001
951—dc21

                                                                                    00-047588

The text of this book is set in 12-point Bembo.

Manufactured in the United States of America

June 2001

10 9 8 7 6 5 4 3 2 1

BVG

To
Victoria and Michael

ACKNOWLEDGMENTS

I thank the following people for being there for me as I was in the process of bringing this memoir to life:

My beautiful wife, Sunni, who told me to write this book, taught me how to write it, and worked tirelessly as a brilliant first editor for it, our third child. This is our book!

Victoria, our daughter, for letting me grow with you. Michael, our son, for your great-grandpa's smiling eyes.

My literary agent, Elaine Koster. You are a superagent.

Ann Godoff, editor-in-chief, publisher, and president of Random House: never a day goes by without my thanking God for you.

Marissa Walsh and Fiona Simpson for your editorial and artistic vision.

And lastly, Beverly Horowitz of Random House Children's Books. Thank you for loving this book and making it into a gift to all the children of the world.

FOREWORD

Volumes have been written about China's Cultural Revolution, which lasted from 1966 to 1976, the time of my childhood. Each account is a horrifying testimony to a time gone bad at the hand of a demonic leader. During Mao Tse-tung's crazy drive to purge all his political enemies, millions died bloodily and many more were wrongly imprisoned. Factories were closed as workers rushed into the streets to shout "Long live Chairman Mao," and schools were shut as Mao stirred youngsters to beat up their teachers, burn down the temples and destroy the ancient arts, and even turn against their own parents in the devilish hunt for more victims.

Books were trashed and classrooms ruined. Factories stood eerily quiet, weeds growing out of cracks in the walls. School campuses became brutal battlefields. Young students, armed with rifles, became roamers jumping on trains, traveling all over the country, toppling buses that would not take them, storming food stores that would not serve them. Fear and hopelessness gripped us all.

The Chinese say curses always come in pairs. During that time, China was also plagued by a desperate famine, and people were dying. Hungry people ate anything—weeds, grass, tree bark, shoe soles, snakes, rats, dogs, cats, other people.

Children crawled naked in the dirt, grabbing anything they could lay their hands on—rotten worms, dead insects, bad fruit, and decayed vegetables.

But the fire of revolution burned on relentlessly. And in the dark shadows of ghostly ashes lived a boy who survived to write this book, a book about love in the face of hate, a book of hope for the hopeless.

Da Chen

ONE

I was born in southern China in 1962, in the tiny town of Yellow Stone. They called it the Year of Great Starvation. Chairman Mao had had a parting of the ways with the Soviets, and now they wanted all their loans repaid or there would be blood, a lot of it.

Mao panicked. He ordered his citizens to cut down on meals and be hungry heroes so he could repay the loans. The superstitious citizens of Yellow Stone still saw the starving ghosts of those who had died during that year chasing around and sobbing for food on the eve of the spring Tomb-Sweeping Festival.

That year also saw a forbidding drought that made fields throughout China crack like wax. For the first time, the folks of Yellow Stone saw the bottom of the Dong Jing River. Rice plants turned yellow and withered young.

Dad wanted to give me the name Han, which means "drought." But that would have been like naming a boy in

Hiroshima Atom Bomb. And since the Chinese believe that their names dictate their fate, I would have probably ended up digging ditches, searching for water in some wasteland. So Dad named me Da, which means "prosperity."

The unfortunate year of my birth left a permanent flaw in my character: I was always hungry. I yearned for food. I could talk, think, and dream about it forever. As an infant, I ate with a large, adult spoon. I would open wide while they shoveled in the porridge. My grandmother said she had never seen an easier baby to feed.

Ours was a big family, and I was at the bottom. There were a great many people above me, with, at the top, my bald, long-bearded grandpa and my square-faced, large-boned grandma. Dad looked mostly like Grandma, but he had Grandpa's smiling eyes. Mom seemed very tiny next to my broad-chested dad. Sister Si was the eldest of my siblings, a big girl who took after Dad in personality and physique. Jin, my brother, had Mom's elegant features; we still haven't figured out just who my middle sister, Ke, looks like. Huang, who is a year older than me, grew up to be a tall, thin girl, a beauty with enormous eyes.

We lived in an old house that faced the only street in Yellow Stone. Our backyard led to the clear Dong Jing River, zigzagging like a dragon on land. The lush, odd-shaped Ching Mountain stood beyond the endless rice paddies like an ancient giant with a pointed hat, round shoulders, and head bent in gentle slumber.

We rarely left our house to play because Mom said there were many bad people waiting to hurt us. When I did go out to buy food in the commune's grocery store a few blocks away, I always walked in the middle, safely flanked by my three sisters as we hurried in and out. Neighborhood boys sometimes threw stones at us, made ugly faces, and called us names. I always wondered why they did that. It was obviously not for fun. My sisters often cried as we ran and dodged and slammed our door shut behind us.

I once tried to sneak through our side door and join the kids in the street, but Si caught me by the arm and snatched me back, screaming and kicking. She gave me quite a spanking for breaking the do-not-go-out order. When I asked Mom why we had to hide in our dark house all the time, she said that we were landlords, and that the people outside were poor peasants who had taken our house, lands, and stores.

They were making us suffer because the leaders were all bad. There was no fairness, no justice for us. We had to be quiet, stay out of trouble, and wait for better days to come.

When? I would ask. Someday, when you grow up, she'd answer. That will be a long time from now, I'd say. Mom would nod, her eyes gently studying my face as if looking for an answer herself. Then she'd take me in her arms and hum her favorite tune—a simple melody urging a boy to eat more and grow up faster so that he could help plow the land with his dad and harvest the grain.

Restricted to the house, I would silently wander into Grandpa's smoky room and practice calligraphy with him. Some days, when my sisters were in school and Mom was busy and not watching me, I would wander out and wrestle with the neighborhood boys. This was a lot of fun, and I would come back all dusty and tell Mom I had fallen, and she would make me change my clothes.

One day when I was about six I stood on the pavement watching a parade of Red Guards carrying their rifles and red flags and shouting slogans, when a kid from next door, for no obvious reason, smacked me right on the face and kicked me when I fell. I picked myself up and charged like a bull into my smiling attacker. When he went down, I straddled him and hit him hard on the face and neck. Within half an hour, the Communist party secretary, a thin little man, stormed into our house with the kid's mother. He started shouting at my mom, demanding to see my father, who was away at labor camp. I hid behind a big chair.

"What have you been teaching your kids, to fight the world? To fight Communism?" He shook his fist at my tiny mom. "I could put you in a labor camp too, if you let one of your kids do this again. Do you hear me?" Mom was too busy crying and being nervous. She didn't answer him right away and the secretary took this as an insult. He slapped her across the face, sending her whirling into a corner. I wanted to jump out from behind the chair and hit him with my fists, but fear held me back. I couldn't afford to bring any more trouble to our family. After spitting his dark phlegm on our spotless floor, the man stormed out. Mom sat there, crying. I spent the rest of the day watching her hold a wet towel to her face, where the humiliating imprint of his hand remained. She was quiet. She had nothing more to teach me about the cruelty outside.

Grandpa, who liked to drink a little—to calm his bones, as he put it—saw no future for us. In school, my sisters sat in the back, although, given their height, they should have been in the middle. They couldn't sing in the choir. They couldn't perform in the school plays. The kids could beat them, spit on them, and the teachers would not say a thing.

Grandpa wished he would die soon in the hope that they might treat us better. Dad said that was nonsense. We were fine the way we were.

But everything wasn't fine. We had been stripped of all our property.

Dad was fired from his teaching job, leaving a family of nine with no income. We relied entirely on a small food ration that went up and down with the harvest each year. A drought could wipe out half a year's ration, and a wet season would rot the young rice in the fields.

For months we would have nothing to eat but tree bark and the roots of wild plants. Even a good harvest would only get us through eight to nine months of the year. The remaining months were called "the season where the green and yellow did not meet." During those months, Dad would be out imploring for a longer grace period on an old loan, and begging to try to borrow more money in order to pay back the debt so that they wouldn't take away the table and chairs. He had already sold the wooden doors and door-frames inside our house to pay for food. Each door was replaced with makeshift planks of rotten wood. But never a day went by without Mom teaching us that we should have dignity in the face of hardship. She would point out to us which land and storefronts used to be ours, and we would feel quietly proud.

For those long months when there was no food, we ate anything that came to our table. One year, we ate moldy yams three times a day for four months. Brother Jin summed it up well when he said, "I'm sick of the yams, but I'm afraid they'll run out." We learned to live with little and be content with what we had. Even the soupy yams brought laughter to our dining table when everyone was there. But most of the time Dad was away at labor camp, or Grandpa was being detained in the commune jail, waiting for another public humiliation meeting to be held in the market square, where he would be beaten badly.

Mom taught us to beg Buddha for his protection and help. This was easier than potty training. All you needed to do was wash yourself really clean, button your buttons, get on your knees, and bang your head on the floor before the hidden shrine of the big, fat, smiling Buddha. Ask all you want to ask and you will be answered, Mom told us.

I followed her to the shrine every day—the shrine that was hidden behind a window curtain in the attic, because religion was not allowed in Communist China. I knelt behind Mom and banged my head on the floor noisily, whispering my small requests. My list grew from two items to many. I asked for Dad not to get beaten by the Red Guards, for Grandpa to be well, for Mom not to cry as much. My last request was always for food—more of it, please.

TWO

造

Yellow Stone Elementary School sat a mile away down the street. It was an old Confucian temple with tilted roofs and lots of wood carvings on the walls. Ancient trees shielded the buildings from the sun, and there was a pond full of lotus blossoms.

When registration day came for the new school year, I got up early and studied my appearance in front of a piece of mirror, broken off from my brother's bigger one. I was as dark as charcoal and as thin as sugarcane. My crew cut, Mom's handiwork, had uneven furrows left behind by rusty scissors and a not-too-experienced hand, as though a clumsy farmer had plowed the fields. I didn't mind it too much. The hair would grow again and the pain of having your hair yanked out by blunt scissors was soon forgotten. My sisters cut each other's hair and Mom took care of the four men in the family. We saved a lot of money that way.

The skin on my forehead was peeling like a snake casting

its skin in the springtime. I rubbed hard and pulled off the larger pieces, but I finally gave up. I would grow out of this terrible tan when the scorching summer changed to a mild, breezy autumn, with deep blue skies and thin white clouds that chased each other like lovers.

I put on a white shirt—a hand-me-down from Jin—and ran to school. The red poster in the schoolyard said that Mr. Sun was to be our new teacher. The tuition was three yuan, a staggering amount on the Chen economic scale. I checked the information twice, wrote it down for Mom to read, and parked myself by the window, watching parents take their kids by the hand and march happily to the teachers to register. It was an all-cash deal. They came out laughing, the kids jumping up and down with a bunch of new books in their hands. It was all cozy for them, but I had to find some resources for my education. I knew well enough that we would be out of rice and yams in a matter of weeks. Dad was away at camp and the food ration kept going down each day. Mom was saving every fen for food. There was no money for tuition. The three yuan I needed would buy us ten pounds of rice, or a hundred pounds of yams. How much knowledge could it buy? I went home with a lump in my throat. I knew the routine well. I would go to Mom and tell her about the tuition. She would tell me how much money she had left for the whole family, a few yuan at most. She would say to go ask for an extension or a waiver of tuition.

Then I would have to go meet my new teacher, begging on my knees.

Even if an extension were granted, the teacher would mention the tuition fees every day in class until everyone would know how poor I was. He might even keep me after school, lecturing. It had happened to my siblings, and all the while they would be going to school without textbooks. Kind students would let them copy from their books. Now it was happening to me.

I went home, feeling defeated, poor, and pathetic. Mom knew why.

She wiped her wet hands on her apron and gave me fifty fen and told me it was a stretch for the family already. I didn't need to be told. A poor child knew what it meant to be poor. We didn't ask for much, and sometimes we didn't even ask.

She said that I should beg for an extension. I asked her just how long would the delay be. She said until the piglets were grown and sold to the buyer from the south. That was something to hope for, but the mother pig was still pregnant. I took the money with a heavy heart. It was a pound of flesh off the family fortune, but only a small piece of the tuition.

I pinned the fifty fen to the inside of my pocket lest I lose them, and ran back to school. I parked myself below the window again and had a good look at the teacher. He was a thin man with short, curly hair like feathers. He seemed your regular, boring, stiff-necked young educator who had read some books. He was shaking hands with the parents of my classmates, smiling and smoking.

I slumped against the wall, feeling depressed. The world was unfair.

Everyone in my class seemed to have young parents with money. They chatted, laughed, and socialized with the new teacher. Their manners were smooth, their clothes were nice. It was a very special occasion for them and a milestone for the kids. Some of the parents were so influential in the little, deprived town of Yellow Stone that being the teacher for those kids could mean a lot of backdoor favors.

And what did I have to offer? Nothing. Grandpa was dying, sick in bed. The doctor said he might live a few months with the proper medication. Tough luck. Medicine was expensive. No money, no life. Dad was digging in the mountains somewhere, camped in an old, windy temple. And I had only fifty fen in small coins. My personal appearance was shocking—a pumpkin head and a ten-year-old patched shirt.

And I personally hadn't eaten any meat since New Year's Day.

The thoughts tortured me and I squirmed in shame and humiliation, but I had to face reality. The teacher could throw me out with a sneer on his face. That was fine, I had thick skin. A poor child couldn't afford to have thin skin. Only rich boys and well-to-do girls with cute little butterflies in their hair could afford to have thin skin.

I adjusted my belt, made sure my fly wasn't open, and gingerly stepped into the teacher's office. I would go there and beg, though I was prepared for the worst. The window looked reasonably large and there was a patch of soft grass for landing.

"So you are Chen Da," he said, to my surprise.

"Yes, sir. I have a problem."

"Don't we all."

"Excuse me?"

"I meant, we all have problems." He was smiling.

"Yes, well, you see, I only have fifty fen for the tuition . . ."

"And you want to register?"

"If I could."

"What's your story?"

"We're waiting for the piglets to grow."

"How big are the pigs?"

"Young."

"How young?"

"Not born yet." I waited for him to grab my neck and toss me out.

"Okay, write a note down here about the pigs and I will register you." I looked at him in disbelief. A wave of gratitude swept through my heart. I wanted to kneel down and kiss his toes. There *was* a Buddha somewhere up there in the fuzzy sky. I took his pen and wrote the promise on a piece of paper.

"But I cannot give you the textbooks now. It's a school rule."

"That's fine. I can copy them from others."

"Well, if you don't mind, I was thinking maybe you could use my last year's copy, but it's messy, it has my handwriting all over the pages." If I didn't mind? Who was this guy? A saint from Buddha's heaven? I was overwhelmed and didn't know what to say. I kept looking at my feet. I had rehearsed being thrown out the window, being slighted or laughed at, but kindness? . . . I wasn't prepared for kindness. I nodded quickly and ran off after saying a very heartfelt thank-you and bowing so deep that I almost rubbed my nose on my knees.

Mr. Sun, the new teacher, came from a village at the foot of the Ching Mountain. He had a sunny personality and was an outdoors kind of guy. In the morning, he and his wife watered the vegetables; then he walked to school. I soon began to tag along behind him like his shadow every morning. He told me many stories during those walks.

He elected me to be the monitor of the class, a bold political decision on his part, and had me lead the revolutionary songs at the beginning of every lesson. I was that one-percent exception in our harsh reality.

I was never supposed to be a leader among other students. I was born with a political defect that no one could fix. But once in a while they threw a bone out to us, a bone that we chased around with enthusiasm.

I was grateful for this bone. I played with it, poked it with my snout, and cherished every moment of being tempted before I sank my teeth into the juiciest part.

I'd arrive early with the teacher and hit the books. In my spare time, I helped the slower students catch up. I was the captain of our basketball team and a formidable singer in schoolwide competitions. Once I sang so loudly that I was hoarse for the next three days. I read classical stories to the whole room while my teacher sat in the back and graded the homework, stopping occasionally to nod with approval.

Late in the afternoons, my new friends—Jie, Ciang, and a few others—would urge me to tell them some more stories. We would climb over the short wall in the back of our school and throw ourselves into an ancient orchard. It was a little paradise.

Our spot was a huge lychee tree with low-hanging boughs. Each of us had a favorite sitting spot. Mine had a back support and a small branch to rest my feet on. The comfort helped the flow of the story.

Sometimes Jie would rub the soles of my feet, which was good for another twenty minutes. And each time I threatened to end the story, they would beg for more and more, and I would have to stretch my imagination and make a short story longer and a long story go on forever.

My popularity went unchallenged till one day a big-eyed boy showed up at our door for late registration. I hated to admit it, but he was good-looking. He was there for five minutes and the girls were already giggling at his sweet smile and nasty winking. During break, I sat in my seat, heaving with anger and contempt for this sudden intruder. I contemplated the proper step to take. I thought of going to him and introducing myself as the leader of the class. It was, after all, my territory, and I deserved a certain courtesy and respect from him. You can't just walk in and ruin everything. If he was a decent man (my keen observation of him during the last hour made me feel this was unlikely) then I would give my blessing, offer my protection, and help him settle in on our turf.

I was, after all, a nice guy with a big heart. I welcomed any bright man as my friend, but no way was I going to walk up to him and shake hands.

He was surrounded by a fan club, admirers who were fawning over something he was wearing. The girls lingered and giggled. The place was out of control.

As I burned with jealousy, a negative feeling that as a leader I tried hard to suppress, the hotshot kid broke through the crowd and walked over. He looked straight at me with those attractive, intelligent eyes of his. At that moment, my heart softened. No wonder the girls had lost their minds. I couldn't help being impressed by the clarity and sense of purpose in his eyes, that straight nose, so sculptural and defined, and that square, chiseled jaw. Had he been a general, I would have followed him into battle and fought until the end.

I stood up with what little dignity I had left and extended my hand to meet his. We shook hands. That was when I saw the buckle. He had this shining buckle the size of a large fist that he wore around his waist.

There were five stars carved on it. It shone in the morning sun, obviously the result of a lot of polishing by a proud hand.

"I heard you're the *Tau-Ke*." The top man.

"Hardly, hardly." High praise called for a humble response, but I was flattered nonetheless.

"I think this would look really good on you." He took his belt and buckle off and handed them over to me, just like that.

"No, no. You wear it."

"I've been wearing it since my dad came back from the Vietnam War." He had the casual art of name-dropping down pat.

"Your dad was in the war with the Americans?"

"Sure, he has lots of medals and was at Ho Chi Minh City. White Americans. Okay, okay, okay." He even spoke English.

He studied the buckle carefully. A wall of classmates had gathered behind me, watching the exchange.

"That belt has a little history to it," he continued.

"What history?"

"My dad wore it in the war. It's been hit a few times but it's so strong and tough you can't even see a dent. I'm talking the superbullets from the American weapons." I was sold on the spot. He became my best friend and we named him Mr. Buckle. He took the nickname in stride.

One day Mr. Buckle formally invited me to visit his home. I accepted and found myself standing before the threshold of a grand town house near the hospital. His dad was the party secretary of the hospital, enjoying a hero's retirement at an early age. The door of the house opened suddenly, and there stood Mr. Buckle senior. Tall and handsome, a man's man. He had a big smile, large eyes, and thick eyebrows, a picture-perfect hero. It was obvious where the son had gotten his good looks.

"Come on in, Da." The father even knew my name.

"Thank you." I extended my right hand but he didn't take it. Instead, he smiled and said, "Sorry, I got no hands left to shake yours. Hey, why don't you shake my shoulder." He leaned over, letting his two empty sleeves dangle, and waited for me to shake his broad shoulder.

I was so shocked at his armlessness that I stood there unmoving.

"That's okay, Dad. I don't think they practice shoulder-shaking in Yellow Stone."

"All right, then. Let's cut the ceremony and have some cookies and candy."

"Dad, we're not babies anymore. Let me show the guy around, okay? I think he has seen enough of you." Father and son bantered back and forth like a couple of drinking buddies while I stood by in deep shock. For Buddha's sake, the perfect hero had no arms. My heart was saddened. Like a lost soul, I followed Buckle around the house and the hospital. He took me on a tour, but my mind was still on those arms. I had no appetite when I went home.

My jealousy was gone. From then on, I quietly watched out for Buckle.

Before long, Mr. Sun was bidding us a sad good-bye. He was heading for a reeducation camp for teachers. I gave him a small notebook as a gift. The school would be taught by the militiamen and women from the commune. There was a directive from the central government that from now on all schools would be governed by poor farmers; all teachers—a class made up of dangerous and stinking intellectuals—would be reformed and instilled with revolutionary thoughts before they could return to teach China's younger generation.

School wasn't the same. Our teacher was a sleepy young man, a distant nephew of Yellow Stone commune's party secretary. He had never graduated from elementary school; he misspelled simple words and twisted pronunciations so badly that they hardly sounded like Chinese anymore. The first day he came to class he was shaking, and there were long lulls while he searched through his notes and tried to think of something to say. In the evening, these farmer teachers played poker and drank at the same tables where real teachers used to grade homework. The zoo was being run by the animals themselves.

To say the least, I was disappointed. I searched outside school for books to entertain myself and yearned for the farmers to leave, to have the real teachers come back from the camp. Although the earliest that could ever happen would be the following year, I nonetheless believed that, like the spring, it *would* happen.

THREE

In September 1971, I entered third grade. Dad had come back from the camp on the mountain and was at another reform camp ten miles away from our town. They made him dig ditches from morning to night to expand an irrigation system that eventually failed to work, while continuing to press for more confessions about my uncle in Taiwan, which had always been China's sworn enemy.

Sometimes I was allowed to visit Dad and bring him food. I would stand on the edge of the work site, searching for signs of my father among the hundred or so other people being "reformed." Tired, curious faces would look at me, word would pass on down the line, then eventually out would come my dad from the ditches, his back straight, head held high, and a dazzling smile on his face for his son as he busily dusted off his ragged clothes. I would have nothing to say and could only look at his blistered hands, while he asked how everybody was and how my schoolwork was going. Then it was time to leave; if I delayed, the foreman would chase me off the site with his wooden stick.

Grandpa was suffering all the time now. An expensive medication was bought to cure him, but he was outraged when he heard its price, since he knew that what it cost could have bought the whole family some decent food for a month. Despite his frail condition, he was still ordered to go to the rice fields every day to chase the birds.

My eldest sister, Si, had graduated from junior high school. Brother Jin had had to stop one year short of completing it, and Ke and Huang were asked to leave before finishing elementary school. When the Red Guards took over the classrooms, they had made the lives of landlords' children and grandchildren miserable. Si's classmates had hacked at her hair with scissors, which made her look like a mental case, and Jin, while he was still in school, had been constantly hassled and beaten by his classmates.

One day we received a notice from the local school authorities. It read, "Due to overcrowding in our school system, it has been decided by the Communist party that the children of landlords, capitalists, rich farmers, and the leftists will no longer be going directly to junior high or high school. This new policy is to be implemented immediately for the benefit of thousands of poor farmers." The curt notice didn't explain the logic behind such a decree. But we understood that they considered us the enemy and a danger to their world. Education could only further our cause and threaten theirs.

Thus I became the last student in our family. Every day Mom would whisper to me before school that I should cherish this precious opportunity. I should work hard and be a good student, or I would have to stop school like my siblings and become a farmer or a carpenter, with no hope for a better future. She said the more they wanted you out of school, the more you should show them how good you are. She admonished me to behave myself and not give them reason to throw me out.

The pressure weighed heavily on me. The idea of being a farmer for the rest of my life, working in the fields unceasingly, rain or shine, chilled my bones. I saw my sisters and brothers, still so young, getting up before dawn to cut the ripened rice in darkness before the biting sun made work unbearable. They came home by moonlight after laboring a full day, their backs cramped and sore, cuts on their fingers, blisters covering their hands. Sometimes they were humiliated because the older, more experienced farmers in the commune trashed them for making mistakes. And sometimes they were angry because they were made to work the heaviest jobs, like jumping into manholes to scoop up manure. At night, my sisters often cried in Mom's arms. They were no longer children.

I looked at school in a different light. It was still a fun place, but now it was much, much more. It was the key to a bright future. I knew if I could somehow stay in school, I would do well. There was hope. I arrived at school early every morning and volunteered to sweep the classroom and clean the blackboard. I still managed to have my morning reading assignment done before the others arrived so that I had time to play and help those who needed some tutoring. But the new teacher wasn't the least impressed with me. I sometimes became aware of him staring silently at my back as I sat alone in class doing my work.

He was cool and abrupt and seemed disgusted with the little boy who wanted so hard to please him.

My third-grade teacher was a young man about twenty-five years old. He had icy, protruding eyes and thin lips that squeezed out his words slowly and deliberately. His nose was pointed, with long, black hairs sticking out of both nostrils, and his receding chin melted into his long neck. He had a habit of looking at his reflection in the window, preening and recombing his hair before entering the classroom.

His name was La Shan.

La Shan invited many of his students to his dormitory on campus, where they played chess and talked long after school. He also organized basketball games among the students, but I was never included. I stood at a distance, watching them play with the energetic young teacher, laughing and shouting. When I inquired about what they did in his dormitory, my friends Jie and Ciang would tell me that they played and listened to La Shan talk about politics, about things like the class struggle and what to do with bad people like landlords and American special agents.

I became quieter and less active in his class. He continued to act as if I didn't exist, and I became more and more isolated, but I still carried on my work with pride and always scored the best in quizzes. I missed my teacher, Mr. Sun, terribly.

In the back of each classroom there was another blackboard on which the best poems or compositions by the students were displayed.

It was an honor to have your work posted, and mine used to appear there every week. Many years under my grandfather's tutelage had made me the best calligrapher in the entire school, and I had won schoolwide competitions against older students. But since La Shan had become my teacher, my work never appeared on the blackboard.

He also deprived me of the task of copying the poems

onto the blackboard with chalk, a task only students with the best calligraphy were allowed to do.

I was no longer the head of the class. In my place stepped the son of the first party secretary of Yellow Stone commune, the most feared man in town. La Shan also made him the head of the Little Red Guard, a political organization for children. I was the only one in class who was not a member. I coveted the pretty red bands worn on their arms and had applied to join, but La Shan told me I needed to make more of an effort, that he wasn't sure I was loyal in my heart to the Communist cause like other children from good working-class families.

Whenever a Little Red Guard meeting was held, I was asked to step outside. I would hang around the playground by myself until they finished.

Because I was driven and still confident in my abilities, I worked even harder and volunteered even more for tasks before and after school. It was like throwing myself against a stone wall. The harder I tried, the more the teacher disliked me. He even criticized me in front of all the students about my overzealous attempts to win his praise. This upset and confused me. What more could I do to try to fit into the place that I once used to love? My first real brush with La Shan came when he was collecting the weekend homework. The assignment had been to copy a text of Chairman Mao's quotations, but my work had been soaked in the rain on the way to class and I had thrown away the smeared, useless paper, intending to redo it in the afternoon. When he found out I had nothing to turn in, La Shan called the class to attention. "Students, Chen Da has not done his homework, which he knew was to copy the text of our great Chairman Mao. It is a deliberate insult to our great leader."

"I did the homework like I always do," I protested loudly, "but the rain got it all wet." The whole class looked at me quietly.

La Shan turned red, the muscles in his cheeks twitching. He had lost face because I had answered back.

"What did you do with it?" he demanded.

"I threw it into a manhole on my way to class because it was all messy." The students laughed.

"*What* did you say?"

"I said I threw it into a manhole," I screamed back. I knew I was acting irrationally but couldn't stop.

"You threw Chairman Mao's quotations into a stinking manhole?" His face flamed and spittle flew from his mouth with each word. "Do you realize how severe an offense you have just committed?" A deadly quiet came over the class. Everyone looked at me, waiting for my reaction. In that split second, I glimpsed the possible serious trouble he could make if he chose to. Mom's words, "Stay out of trouble," rang in my ears.

I felt dizzy, as if I had been hit with a club. I already regretted my actions and wished I could take everything back, but it was too late, the damage had been done. I thought of Mom and Dad and the trouble I might have just brought to my family if the teacher blew this thing up.

My head began to pound.

"I am sorry, honorable teacher. I will redo my homework and hand it in as soon as possible."

He stared at me silently with his icy eyes, looking like a wolf that had just caught a rabbit in a trap.

"You think it's going to be that easy?" He shook his head slowly.

"Everybody!" His voice cracked out. "Let's have a vote.

Those who wish to have Da thrown out of our classroom, raise your hands." There was a moment of silence. Then slowly, the son of the party secretary raised his hand. A few more hands from the La Shan club went up. Next the whole class raised their collective hands, even my friends Jie and Ciang.

I felt trapped. I felt half-dead. I couldn't understand how even my best friends could vote against me.

"Please, I don't want to leave this class. I would like to stay."

"We'll see about that. Class is over for the day," La Shan said, slamming his book closed and walking out of the room, his disciples trailing behind him.

I walked home in a daze. Nobody talked to me. I redid my homework and turned it in right away. I waited for La Shan to throw me out of school, but nothing happened. I sat in the back corner of the class by myself. No one talked to me, not even my friends. Occasionally, La Shan would throw disgusted glances my way. The worst thing was when he disparagingly called me "that person in the corner" without looking at me. Why did he take the whole thing so personally, as if I had desecrated his ancestors' tombstone? Then one day during the morning exercise break La Shan called my name and asked me to stay behind while the others noisily poured out of class.

"I have received reports about you," he said, pacing in front of the classroom. "Really bad reports."

My heart began to race. "What kind of reports?"

"You have been saying antirevolutionary and anti-Communist things to your classmates, haven't you?"

"No, I haven't." He was trying to paint me as a counter-revolutionary, just as they had done to Yu Xuang, a fifth-grader whom they had locked in the commune jail for further investigation. It was a dangerous situation.

"I have never done anything like that! You know that!" I said, using the best defense a nine-year-old could muster.

"I have the reports here"—he waved a thick sheaf of paper—"and I can ask these people to testify against you if necessary."

"The people who wrote those reports were lying. I have never said anything against our country or the Communist party."

"Shut up! You have no right to defend yourself, only the chance to confess and repent," he spat out angrily. His voice deepened. "Do you understand what kind of trouble you are in now?"

"I have nothing to confess!" I was losing control again. My throat dried up and my arms began to tremble.

"I said, shut up! You have today and tonight to write a confession of all the treasonous things you have said, to explain the motivation, and to state who told you to say these horrible things. Like perhaps your father, mother, or your landlord grandparents." He was trying to involve my family. They would put my dad in prison. They would take Grandpa out into the street and beat him to death.

"They did *not* tell me to do or say bad things against the party! They didn't!" I cried. I couldn't afford to have my family dragged into this. I was scared and began to sob helplessly. The sky had just caved in and I felt that nobody could help me. I would be a young counterrevolutionary, a condemned boy, despised by the whole country. I would be left to rot in a dark prison cell for life. That was what had happened to Shi He, another high school kid, who was caught listening to an anti-Communist radio program from Taiwan, and worse, to the banned Teresa Deng's love songs. His prison sentence had been twenty years.

I don't remember how long I cried that morning. When I walked home alone in the afternoon's setting sun, I felt the weight of shackles already around my ankles.

A condemned man at the age of nine! Confession tomorrow! The thoughts played over and over in my mind.

When I got home, I told Mom what had happened and she started sobbing, hitting her face and chest and pulling out her hair. She mumbled hysterically, in broken sentences, that their generation had brought the curse to the next generation. After a while, she sat down quietly, weak and limp like a frightened animal. Finally, she got up and sent Si and Jin to Dad's camp to ask for advice. They got to talk to him by using the excuse that Mom was very sick again.

It was after midnight when, breathless, they ran back. I was still sitting in my room, staring at a piece of blank paper. I had not eaten anything. For the first time in my life, I had absolutely no appetite.

The message from Dad was simple. There was nothing to confess.

Go back to school tomorrow and tell them that, he instructed. What were they going to do to you? Nothing, if you did not confess. Everything, if you did. If school becomes too hard, then quit. Dad's words gave us power and courage even from afar, allowing me to feel hopeful again that everything would be fine. But I dreamed that night of the teacher's face and smelled the dank odor of a dark, wet prison.

The following day, I dragged myself along the cobbled street, my eyes fixed on the ground, wishing I were as tiny as a mosquito. When I entered the classroom, there were silent stares from the other children.

The lesson was on fractions, but nothing sank in. My mind kept wandering to the piece of paper I carried with me. What would the teacher say? What were they going to do to me? Each hour of class crawled torturously by. I couldn't wait to hand in the confession and run back home to my family.

Finally, the day came to an end. My classmates filed out as I put my books in my schoolbag and prepared to face the teacher.

"You're not going anywhere, are you?" La Shan questioned sternly, not looking up from the homework he was grading.

"I was just going to give you this." I pulled out the piece of paper. "May I come up to your desk, please?"

"You have your confession?" he asked sharply, arching his eyebrows.

"I thought long and hard, and all that I have to say is here, honorable teacher." I put the "confession" on his desk and turned to walk away.

"Stop!" His voice was so angry and disgusted it startled me. I stopped and stood there with my head down, afraid to look at him.

"You confessed nothing?" he screamed at me. "Did your parents tell you to write this?" He crushed the paper into a ball and threw it at me.

"No, it is all from me and it is the truth. I swear upon my ancestors' graves that I am honest and innocent." Tears trickled uncontrollably down my face. I was so nervous that my head began to feel hot again.

Desperately, I felt myself losing my logic and calm.

"You are a liar, Chen Da! I am going to refer your counterrevolutionary acts to the principal and party secretary of the school. I wished to handle your case here, but you are not cooperating, so now you force me to go to higher authorities."

The teacher dropped me off in the principal's office and left. The principal didn't even bother to look at me. He was cleaning his huge wooden desk as I stood nervously in the corner.

The principal, Mr. Gao, was a frog of a man. He had bowed legs and walked with a wide side-to-side swing. Despite a mustache, his face was bland. He was about fifty and, in addition to being the school principal, had recently been promoted to the position of party secretary.

Older students once told me that he loved fondling little girls' hands and shoulders and enjoyed having young female teachers iron his clothes in his dormitory room late at night while he conferred his seasoned political wisdom on them. He was the most zealous objector to romance among the young teachers because, it was said, he couldn't bear the idea of anyone else having his way. His wife was a heavy smoker, with yellow teeth and ugly wrinkles on her face. They were a well-matched couple.

He asked me all kinds of questions and urged me again to make a confession. I declared my innocence over and over.

For the entire week that followed, Mr. Gao met with me daily, either in between classes or after school. He went on mumbling his advice and making threats to stop my schooling. I sat quietly during those sessions, much more alert and logical than in the presence of the teacher. Though Mr. Gao was the top dog, he somehow didn't scare me. He muttered rather than talked and he was an incoherent speaker.

He would start a line of argument then totally lose himself in it until he had to ask me blankly, "Where were we?"

Finally, one day he said, "If you do not confess, I am send-ing your case to the commune and the police." This time, his face was deadly serious. "You have left me no other choice. In fact, the police chief asked about you the other day and recommended that you appear on the public humiliation platform with Yu Xuang during his confession in front of the whole school."

Gloomily, I headed for home, hoping there was a god who could turn the whole world around, send me a new, bright day full of colors, but it was hopeless. A family was registered at a certain commune. You couldn't move anywhere else un-less the government reassigned you.

There was no escape.

As the day of Yu Xuang's public denunciation ap-proached, Mom quietly said to me, "Go pack. You are leav-ing tomorrow."

"Where am I going?"

"To Wen Qui's home." He was a distant cousin who lived in Ding Zhuan, another tiny town about twenty miles west of Yellow Stone.

"They will catch me."

"No, they won't come after you. They were just threat-ening you."

"What about school?" It was my future.

"We will worry about that later. You can still be the best student after missing a few lessons."

I went into her arms. "I'm scared."

"Don't be." She held me tight. "Wen Qui has already been secretly informed of your coming." The next day, as the sky shed its first ray of light, I crept out our back door, crossed the wooden bridge that swung and squeaked in the wind, and started my half day's journey on foot. I carried a bag of clothes, a small bag of dried yams to contribute to Wen Qui's household when I got there, and two pieces of sweet rice cake, which was my favorite treat, and which Mom had stayed up late preparing for me. As soon as I crossed the Dong Jing River, I followed Mom's instructions: ducked low and disappeared into the lush milelong field of sugarcane to avoid bumping into anyone. The morning dew still kissed the sharp leaves that innocently scratched my face and arms.

Beyond the sugarcane field lay a narrow dirt road winding into the mountains. Though I had walked this scenic path a few times before, it was scarily quiet in the early dawn, so I sang out loud and whistled as I ran along, my bag bouncing on my back. When I was halfway to my destination I sat down to rest by a large pond. I leaned against an old pine tree and unwrapped my first piece of rice cake. As I sank my teeth into the sticky sweet rice, I was reminded once more of how good life could be if one weren't a political fugitive running for his life.

I took off my shoes and waded in at the shallow edge of the pond, scooping up a handful of the fresh springwater to drink. It tasted as sweet as the mountain itself. Everything was so peaceful I couldn't help skipping a few rocks and watching the ripples spread out gently. I remembered the time my dad and I competed at this very pond to see who could skip a rock the farthest. I had thrown a stone so hard that I had skidded and fallen into the soft young wheat, and now, again, I could hear Dad's hearty laughter at my antics.

When I got to the Quis' home, it was lunchtime. Wen's sister was the wife of my uncle. The family had been forced to move to this small mountain village remote from Yellow Stone because his father had been a wealthy fabric merchant. Wen once said his father could judge the quality of a fabric by blindly feeling it behind his back. The Quis lived in the house of a former landlord, a man whose family had all been executed by the Communists.

I stayed there for a week before it was deemed safe for me to return.

I heard that at the public humiliation meeting Yu Xuang was sentenced to four years of labor reform in a juvenile prison. He was beaten unconscious after being thrown off the stage. No one had come to inquire about me.

Mom said later that she had spent the entire day on her knees in front of Buddha, praying for my safety.

FOUR

造

I quit school after I came back from hiding. I kept expecting
the teacher, the principal, or the police chief to show up any
day for my capture. I asked Jie and Buckle, who still talked
to me occasionally, whether they had heard anything about a
public meeting to be held soon in the school. They said no.

I spent my time weeding the sweet potatoes in the fields,
building a dirt wall in our backyard, carrying lunches and
dinners to my brother and sisters in the fields in little bamboo baskets slung over my shoulders, and spreading wet hay
to dry before storing it in the evenings. Bugs crawled everywhere and the moist hay's sharp, bladelike edges made my
skin itch constantly.

As I became more and more settled into the routine of a
young farmhand, part of me was dying inside. I felt old and
rejected, a misfit.

The people I worked with were all older farmers who
could no longer work the fields.

I no longer played. I had aged and had become an outcast. By now, everyone knew the reason why I had quit school.

Sometimes the kids shouted outside my house, calling me the "little counterrevolutionary," daring me to come out and fight them. I would clutch a sharp spade and wait behind the door in case they burst through and attacked us. A few times, stones were thrown against our windows. One morning Mom found a dead bird in our backyard, headless. I suspected the teacher had urged his gang to come after me.

Whenever Mom asked me to run out to buy some soy sauce, I checked the street first, then darted out and back. The last thing I wanted to do was cause any more trouble.

But every night before I went to sleep, I wrote in my diary, trying not to forget the words I had learned. I made up a lot of signs for the words I didn't know. There was nothing good to write about. Often I found myself drawing a picture of La Shan, the chinless skunk, and adding a huge bullet hole on his forehead. Someday I wanted to avenge all the things that had been done to me. Maybe when I grew up or maybe when the world changed.

Then one day a kindhearted teacher named Mr. Lan from our neighborhood dropped by to have tea with us. He casually mentioned that he had brokered a deal with the school to allow me to enter group eight of the fourth grade. He said, smiling, "It's better than being a farmer and genuine pearls shine even in darkness." I remembered that line for a long time.

With mixed feelings of joy, fear, curiosity, and suspicion, I dusted off my books and prepared for the frightening ordeal of going back to face the very same people I had tried to avoid.

On Monday morning, shock hit me as I stepped into the classroom of the fabled group eight. The kids hooted at me. It took me a second before I noticed that the seating arrangement was unlike that in any other classroom. The desks were separated into two corners. One was for eight girls in the front. The other was in the far back corner for the boys. There was a large empty space in the middle of the room where trash and paper planes were piled up.

The teacher gestured with his cigarette in the direction of the boys' group and absentmindedly said, "Pick a chair for yourself over there."

"Which one?" I asked. The dirty faces from the boys' corner looked dangerously back at me.

"Any seat, I said." The teacher, whom I came to know as Mr. Chu, swiped his arm in that general direction again.

I nervously walked down the open space in the middle and took a seat at the edge of the group next to a fat, ugly little guy.

"Whaddya doing here, big shot?" my new neighbor shouted, stretching his arms to mark his territory line on the desk we shared.

Somehow, I had a feeling they knew I had been kicked out of group one, where all the brightest students and the snobs were.

By the second class, I was able to answer eighty percent of the math questions, and by the third, the class had found a new star. At the end of the day, a big guy with a nasty cut, who was known as the King, walked over and patted my shoulder, announcing, "From now on, you can sit next to me and do my homework whenever I feel like it." I was flattered by the intimacy and readily agreed. It wasn't as if I had any choice. The boy was a head taller than me and was surrounded by all his lieutenants, each more devilish than the other. They seemed to be the class Mafia.

That night, lying in bed, I was convinced that I couldn't have found a more nurturing environment to revive my student career. My classmates were animals, but they couldn't care less where I had come from. They respected me.

I considered it a tragedy when group eight was dissolved at the end of the term. A school closer to the villagers reopened and the students happily went back to their own school. I got placed in group two, next door to the hateful faces I tried to erase from my memory forever. Each day I ran past the doors of group one as fast as possible, for fear of bumping into them and getting into trouble. In the new group, I soon became the recognized top student. I began to hear some good words from a few of the teachers. But a gang of students in my new class was organized against me. It was headed by a sneaky boy called Han, whose father had fallen out with mine after a bee-raising business they had started together failed. The others in the gang were Quei, the son of a local politician, and Wang, whose father was a carpenter and an enemy of some of my father's good friends.

During this time, Grandpa was slowly dying. He was seventy-seven years old. Almost every day, I found writings on the blackboard that debased and humiliated him.

On the day he died, we carried him in a wheelbarrow about twenty miles away to the city of Putien for cremation. I wore a white shirt and spread pieces of paper money over the bridges we passed and chanted sayings like "peaceful passing" to the imaginary soldiers guarding the bridges. In the crowd that watched the procession, I saw the three ugly mugs of Han, Quei, and Wang, smiling without pity or sympathy. They even made faces at me. I bit my lips, trying to control my sadness and hatred. Tears poured forth as the strong voice of revenge cried out within me. I wiped away my tears and walked on with my family, pushing Grandpa's body along the dirt road to Putien for two more hours.

When we got there, four young monks were hired to carry Grandpa up the mountain to the cremation site. I knelt before his body with my family like a pious grandson, sobbing farewell as an ancient monk torched the woodpile beneath Grandpa's flimsy coffin. Flames shot up against the setting sun. My beloved Grandpa was no more.

FIVE

Even in wintertime Yellow Stone was laced by the greenness of the surrounding wheat and fava bean fields. Yellow wild-flowers were scattered across the green carpet like solitary souls still searching for their destiny. The water of the Dong Jing River lay calm and pensive, as if quietly dreaming about the coming spring.

Farmers flocked to the market square to trade goods for the new year, a week away. The narrow streets of Yellow Stone became filled with mules carrying food and vegetables. Bicycles strained beneath the double weight of two riders, and noisy tractors fought their way among crowds of people carrying sacks of produce slung over their shoulders.

One morning, Teacher Lan visited our home with the results of our first countywide exam. I had scored 100 percent in all four subjects. He and Mom couldn't stop smiling and my sisters swarmed, fighting to get a glimpse of the report card.

"Only two students made that score in the whole county of Putien," Lan said, beaming happily, for my distinction had made him one of the teachers of the year.

I became an instant star among the neighbors. There were some warmer glances and sweeter greetings for me. It was both liberating and a little intoxicating. I felt glorified. I was no longer just another one of those hopeless descendants of the old ruling class, who ended up becoming a carpenter, a blacksmith, or a nobody, buried in the guilt and shame of his fathers. I shone, despite their efforts to snuff me out.

Early in the morning on New Year's Day, I helped Mom prepare all kinds of sacrifices before our makeshift shrine of numerous gods. There was Buddha, his Kitchen God, the Earth God, Rice God, Water God, and all our dead ancestors. It was pretty much like the administration of a government, Mom explained. There were local gods, provincial gods, and the big Buddha on top. She had designated a spot for each, with different displays of food as sacrifices. There were chicken, fish, shrimp, clams, crabs, whole piglets painted in red, greasy ducks, colored eggs, wine, peaches, pears, bananas, rice, and a lot of incense and paper money to burn.

With incense clutched in her hands, Mom knelt and said the prayers.

I waited on the side and kowtowed as many as fifty to a hundred times before each god, doing extras for my sisters and brother. I couldn't remember how I had gotten into the business of kowtowing for my siblings. All I knew was that I was a little more religious than they were. I had always been afraid of ghosts and believed in the power of good gods. I prayed like a monk and didn't mind bending down on my skinny knees to kowtow as often as Mom thought appropriate, usually imagining a hundred to be her lucky number.

By the end of the ceremonies, though my back and knees ached, I was quietly content with the prospect of having bought my insurance with gods at all levels for the new year to come. I told my sisters and brother that I had also done favors before the gods in their stead and had them pay me back in monetary terms. They believed enough to pay me five fen each.

For breakfast on New Year's Day, long, thin handmade noodles were prepared, served in elegant little bowls and decorated on top with slices of fried egg, marinated meat, fried peanuts, oysters, crispy seaweed, and lightly sautéed crunchy snow peas. Long noodles promised longevity. The word *oysters,* in my local dialect, meant "alive." Eggs were round and perfect. Peanuts indicated countless offspring, and if you twisted the pronunciation of *seaweed* a little, it sounded a lot like the word that meant "fortune."

I fought down the long noodles, donned a new jacket that Mom had tailored herself, and ran off to offer New Year's greetings to our neighbors. I clasped my hands, bowed my head, and wished wealth to the garlic-nosed Liang Qu, an old man with seven sons, who made a living selling cigarettes to children behind closed doors at a huge markup. He wiped his big, dripping nose and threw me a cigarette with dark tobacco in it. "Thanks and happy new year, young fella. Have a smoke," he said.

"It's not one of those moldy ones, is it?" I teased as I pocketed it. He was known to pass the kids rotten products. Since the children were smoking secretly, they never complained. Only on New Year's Day could I get away with a joke like that.

I crossed the bridge to greet the white-haired country

doctor, who peered at me through his thick glasses, trying to figure out who I was.

"I'm the younger son of the Chens," I said.

He nodded, pointed with his cane at the seat next to him, and offered some tea. I politely told him I had just had breakfast. He asked how my grandpa was. "He's gone," I said. I couldn't believe how forgetful the doctor was. Only half a year ago, he had been telling us that Grandpa didn't have long to live.

"Oh, I'm sorry. But the living has to go on, ain't that right?"

"Right, Doctor. Happy New Year." He nodded in silence and watched me run off down the dirt road.

It was a tradition that for good luck you should greet as many people as you could on New Year's Day. To me, it was the easiest way to score brownie points with people, for they were in the best of spirits then and you could get a lot of goodwill for nothing.

By noon, I had greeted no fewer than fifty people. There was the brigade leader, the neighborly Teacher Lan, the kind tailor who sometimes let Mom use his sewing machine, the blacksmith who made good farming tools for us, and the lock-smith who stuttered when he became excited. His son had gone to Chinghua University in Beijing, the equivalent of MIT. He had the hardest time saying the name and always ended up stuttering "Chin . . . Chin . . . Chin . . . Chinghua University." By the time he did the third "hap . . . hap . . . hap" of his unfinished "happy New Year" greeting, I was long gone.

When I got home for lunch, our living room was already filled with well-wishers. Dad was holding court, busily pour-ing hot tea and lighting the water pipe for his visitors.

I often thought that if Dad hadn't been the unfortunate son of a landlord, he probably would have ended up being one of the Communist leaders. He was a big man who commanded attention the moment he entered a room. Dad loved laughing and could charm your boots off, but when he was angry, his temper thundered and his tongue lashed out mercilessly. He was a natural, a dramatic leader in a sleepy little town like Yellow Stone.

The commune leaders put him down like trash; bad neighbors and ignorant militiamen spat in his direction when they passed him in the street. But villagers from the surrounding towns and remote farms still came to him for all sorts of advice. They came in groups of five and ten and treated Dad as if he were still the son of an old family that had once headed the local gentility.

He wrote persuasive letters for those whose relatives resided in rich places like Singapore, Hong Kong, and Malaysia, helping them to squeeze money from their rich relatives. Defenseless widows sought his aid in drawing up complaints about neighbors who had encroached on their properties and families who had abandoned them. They paid Dad with money or a sack of rice or yams. But a lot of advice was offered free, with a smile.

Gradually, Dad's reputation spread, with villagers dropping by daily when they were in town to shop. They came for a cup of hot tea, a puff on the water pipe, or just to rest their feet. If Dad wasn't away at a reform camp, by eleven every morning the living room was always full of all sorts of personalities. Dad felt comfortable in the role and presided over the affairs of others like an unpaid civil servant. The only rule was that there was to be no spitting on the clean floor, which Mom scrubbed daily.

On this special day, all the friendly, familiar faces were crowded into our sun-drenched living room, bubbling with excitement as they lit their good cigarettes. I sat there, as I had for many years, listening to Dad's friends doing their New Year's version of a daily chat for a little bit.

But on New Year's Day, I felt a need for something more festive and entertaining, only there wasn't much I could do. I could just see my enemies, Han, Quei, and Wang, chomping cigarettes and lurking among the crowds, plotting their revenge against me. And I couldn't fight that day; it would be bad luck.

After lunch, when my brother, Jin, was out playing poker and my sisters had long since gone out giggling with their friends, doing whatever girls did, I told Mom I was heading out to a basketball game at school.

"I didn't hear about a game there," Mom said.

"Yeah, well it should be starting soon," I lied, and streaked out the door. I walked cautiously along the small path meandering among the wheat and sugarcane fields, staying away from the crowded streets, which were now filled to the brim with villagers who had flocked to town for the New Year. It was an event locally known as Yu Chun, or Spring Outing. They came in groups of boys and girls, nicely dressed in new and colorful outfits. They sang, laughed, flirted, and ogled each other.

The spring, now ripening with blossoms, seemed to stir a nameless agitation among the youngsters and to give an added luster to the world. I envied the simplicity of their lives. Why was mine so damned complicated? Soon I was alone, looking for a shortcut to the secret gambling pits somewhere among the tall sugarcane fields. Children my age whispered about them and raved over the heroism of some of the big-time winners whenever news mysteriously found its way out of the pit. But none dared venture near the place. A few really bad older boys from our neighborhood were said to make their homes there during the whole New Year's holiday.

If I couldn't have fun in normal places, then I was determined to find something else to do, watching the game or even running errands for those bad boys. I had only brought half a yuan with me. That way if they wanted me in the game, I wouldn't have too much to lose.

I was mentally prepared for any roughing up that might occur.

I checked over my shoulder to make sure nobody was following me, then slipped into the sugarcane field. The leaves were thick and sharp.

I ducked beneath them and walked with bent knees toward the heart of the field.

After ten minutes, I heard vague, hushed voices. Then I suddenly saw lights and a clearing ahead of me. Twenty yards of sugarcane had been felled and trampled down, and there were at least two dozen young people sitting at tables, squatting, and standing in clusters around the cleared area.

I jumped out quickly and they all froze. Their angry faces stared at me as if I had already overstayed my welcome. The only thing moving was the cigarette smoke spiraling over their heads. It was a perfect group picture of the local criminal elite in full swing.

"What are you doing here, you little punk? I thought you were a good mama's boy. This is no place for you," Mo Gong, the local shoemaker's son, barked at me. His diction was crude, his tone menacing. His nostrils flared as he threw his cigarette butt at me. "Get outta here." In the hierarchy of the local criminal elite, he easily took the top spot. He once cut his enemy's shoulder open with a sharp knife meant for trimming rubber-soled shoes.

"Yeah, get outta here," another member of the elite roared.

I covered my head with my arms like a surrendering war criminal and moved slowly around the edge.

Mo Gong took a few steps and threw me to the ground, which was covered with springy crushed sugarcane. He sat on me, twisted my arms behind my back, and demanded, "Who sent you here?"

"Nobody, I just wanted to see what's going on." My nose was being ground against his muddy leather boots.

"Who told you where we were?"

"I found my way here."

"Liar!" He forced my head harder against the ground. It smelled like the pig manure used as fertilizer.

"Wait, Mo Gong, let go of him," I heard a calm voice say from above me. It sounded like Sen, the son of the local banker, the brains behind all the scandals in the recent history of Yellow Stone. Mo Gong did as he was told, but not before kicking me once more on the behind.

I got up and dusted the dirt off my new coat. Sen grabbed Mo Gong and pulled him aside.

"Don't hurt him too much or he'll tell the commune leader and we'll be in trouble," I heard Sen whisper. Then he turned around and grabbed my shoulder.

"I'll let you stay, but don't come back tomorrow and don't tell anyone about this place. If you do, I'll have Mo Gong make you a useless cripple," he warned, his eyes unmoving.

"I just want to watch, that's all."

"Quiet! And I want your mouth shut while you watch,

hear me?" I remained gratefully quiet as I stood far behind the circle. Sen took his place at the head of one of the tables. It was a simple poker game played by four, two against two. The starting bet was half a yuan, which would only give me one shot if I were to jump in.

Two minutes into the game, Sen and his partner, Mo Gong, started making faces, blowing their noses, and cracking their knuckles. They were playing against a couple of out-of-town village boys who didn't know their sign language. Soon the villagers were losing fast, and they wanted out.

"Can't do that in this town." Mo Gong put his dirty palm on their money.

"Says who?" The villagers were a bit taller than they were.

"You guys don't play fair. We're leaving," one of the villagers said as he pushed Mo Gong's hand away and grabbed the money.

"We said at the beginning that the game is finished only when you're empty. I don't think you're empty," Sen said coolly. "Sit down."

"What's this? Are you guys trying to make us stay?" The villagers stepped together, back to back.

Sen and Mo Gong were also on their feet now. I saw Sen make another one of his faces; then he and Mo Gong were on top of them.

Fights must have been common in this place, because the people at other tables didn't even turn around. "Quiet, you guys. Keep it down," they shouted.

The four wrestled on the ground, seemingly inseparable. They went on wrestling like that for five minutes until the pile of money was scattered all over the place. Whenever Sen rolled over to face me, he winked at me, gestured toward the money, and went on fighting.

Finally, I got his message. I looked around and kicked the wads of money between the cracks of trampled sugarcane, where they were hidden among the dense leaves. When the villagers kicked off their shoes, I picked them up and threw them into the fields while they weren't looking.

It was over when they were too tired to fight anymore. The two villagers stumbled around dizzily, looking for their money and shoes, finding neither. Complaining and cursing, they walked out of the pit, never looking back.

As soon as the villagers were out of sight, Sen and Mo Gong burst into laughter. Their faces were covered with mud and bloody cuts; their clothes were torn. They squatted down, looking for the hidden bills. They collected forty or fifty yuan in total.

"Here, take this." Sen stuffed a bunch of small bills into my hands.

"I don't want any."

"Fine, then you don't get any."

"You guys are ruthless," I said.

"Hey, you weren't too bad yourself. I saw you kick the money and throw the shoes away," Sen said with a smile, and pinched my ear.

As I made my way home, I found myself smiling. Those guys were rough but likable. They were natural and up-front, no hidden emotions.

It would be great to learn to smoke, drink, and gamble, and be their friend. I could imagine my enemies' faces. They'd look like spineless little rascals compared to these boys.

SIX

After my first encounter with the gambling duo, Sen and Mo Gong, I had to control the urge to go back and see them the next day.

If I ventured out again so soon, it would arouse suspicion in my family, and then my adventure would end prematurely. I looked out from our second-floor window, trying to get a glimpse of the gambling pit, but all I could see was the cold wind making the sugarcane leaves dance like the ocean waves.

Mom and Dad wanted us to grow up to be perfect kids so that our ugly political birthmark would be obliterated. They hoped one day that all those leaders would wake up and say, "Hey, you guys are a bunch of wonderful kids. C'mon, let's get you into schools and offer you jobs." If we fought against her belief, Mom would cite the example of a girl from a neighboring town. Li Jun too came from a landlord's family, but she had recently been selected by the commune to work in a food canning factory, a juicy plum of a job that any child of a good family would kill to get. She left town on the back of the commune's tractor wearing a big paper flower on her flat chest as she rode down the street of Yellow Stone in all her glory. No one could forget the tears and smiles of joy on her pretty face. She was the one in a thousand that the Communist rulers used to illustrate their benevolent policy toward us.

The message was that if you were obedient, a future might be handed down to you.

We all knew this wasn't true and listened to it as though it were the western wind blowing in one ear and out the other. It made us want to puke. Children like us all over the commune were still getting beaten up and thrown out of school. Even those who had obtained good jobs and had been afforded a college education before the Cultural Revolution were sent back to the town of their birth to become reeducated. Sometimes they were even jailed if they rebelled against local ignorance. Zhu Eng, the son of a counterrevolutionary, was clubbed to death in the bushes by his college classmates at a Shanghai university. All his family received was a jar containing their son's ashes and a police statement saying he had taken his own life and had wasted the government's investment in him.

Mom still disciplined us strictly. Cynicism wasn't allowed in our family. Her belief was that we should do more and get less. When people spit at you, look the other way. When they curse you, pretend to be deaf. If she found out about my visit to the gambling pit, I'd be grounded for at least three days.

But boredom and the need to make friends got the better of me. The next day I took some cigarettes from Dad's drawer and sneaked back to the sugarcane fields.

Mo Gong and Sen treated me coolly, as if they had forgotten our united work such a short time ago. But they smoked my cigarettes and let me try some of theirs. It was the first time I'd smoked with the big league. Mo Gong showed me how to inhale without its hurting too much. Smaller puffs at first, he said. I felt the rush to my head, numbing and soothing at the same time. I washed my mouth with handfuls of water by the river before heading home. Once I got home, I didn't speak until I had had some garlic, onions, and a lot of soup to mask the foul scent.

The second day, Sen let me sit next to him for good luck and showed me the way he handled cards. I was so flattered by his trust I kept on nodding, feigning ignorance of the game.

The third day, Mo Gong wanted me to sit with him and even let me pick the amount to bet. For the rest of the sessions, they coached me on their sign language. They had me standing at another table, opposite their other two friends, Yi and Siang, where I scratched my head and picked my nose to give away their competitors' cards. They kept winning.

The fourth day, I was late in coming to the field.

"Where have you been?" Sen asked. "Come sit here by me. I've been losing too much money without you being here." He ruffled my hair, threw me a whole pack of unopened cigarettes, and let me cut the cards for good luck. As I lit my first cigarette of the day, I smiled. It was very satisfying to be missed by these hooligans.

That evening, after the four of them split their money, I went home, wrapped up some of Mom's sweet rice cakes, and shared them with my new friends. They fought like hungry dogs and ate with dirty hands.

After they were done, they wiped their mouths with the corners of their jackets and ran their greasy hands through their unruly hair so that it would look shiny.

"No matter how shiny your hair is, you still look ugly, Sen," Mo Gong joked.

"You look even worse," Sen retorted, touching his hair.

"Okay, okay, you both look ugly." Siang laughed.

They started hitting each other for fun. Yi grabbed my hair with his greasy hands and we started wrestling. Later, we took a stroll to the marketplace near the theater and used some of the gambling money to buy candies and more cigarettes. We laughed, talked, and joked until midnight. Then, reluctantly, I told them I had to go home. In my household, it was way beyond bedtime, even though it was still the New Year's holiday period. They pushed me around jokingly and Siang lifted me up to his shoulders. Then they said good-bye.

I lay in bed and couldn't go to sleep for a long time. Their laughter, their faces, their way of saying things, and the way they had included me like a real friend replayed in my mind like a colorful film. They had never once mentioned that I was from a landlord's family. They called me "little punk" because I was three or four years younger, weighed twenty pounds less, and measured a head shorter. With them, I felt a freedom to say and do whatever I wanted without worrying that they might report me to the school authorities. My enemies at school looked conniving and petty in comparison. If they thought they were bad, wait till they saw these guys. I drifted off into a sound sleep, hoping tomorrow would come quickly.

As the holiday came to an end, the seasonal gambling activities also died away, once all the New Year's money had been won, lost, and spent. The five of us began to hang out at their usual spots. Their favorite was the stone bridge where the Dong Jing River crossed our narrow street. The thoughtful architect had built a row of stone seats along the bridge, where we would sit in the evenings, chatting and watching townspeople come and go. Mo Gong and Sen would make rude comments to passing females, then laugh like a bunch of monkeys when the girls scolded them and called them ruffians who belonged in jail. My friends seemed to take pleasure in anything that stimulated them, and in making fools of themselves.

Soon I came to know their personalities and the hierarchy that existed within the group. Sen, fifteen, was the lead dog. He had the brains and audacity. He was born the middle brother of five who fought one another at home every day. His dad worked for a bank in a faraway town near the salt factory along the coast, sent money home once a month, and visited every third month. His mom raised the five boys like a single parent. Each day she could be found chasing one of her unruly sons with a long wooden stick, cursing her ancestors for giving her these demons to torture her in this life. She was often busy in the fields doing farmwork, so Sen's elder brother would be in charge of cooking for the family. The cook often ate up most of the food, and whoever came home late got nothing.

Once Sen was detained by the commune's police because someone had accused him of setting fire to a watchman's little hut. When the police came to notify his mother and ask her to take him home, she said, "He's not my son. Do whatever you want with him," and shut the door in the cop's face. The poor officer, who was prepared to give a long lecture to the mother, left confused and disappointed. They let Sen out without a scratch.

Mo Gong, also fifteen, distinguished himself by almost killing someone with a big knife when he was thirteen. Years later, the sheer size of the weapon still shocked people. He grew up in a family of entrepreneurs.

His mom and dad secretly made shoes behind closed doors and sold them in the black market. Mo Gong was born a rough kid and couldn't stay out of trouble. His mouth said the wrong things and his hands were always out of control. He had an endless need to touch and hit things. No matter how hard his parents tried to discipline him, it never worked. They had hung him by the wrists, locked him up, and whipped him till his butt was red and swollen. He always went back to the old ways. He stole money from home to buy cigarettes, liquor, and food.

The reputations of Sen and Mo Gong were so bad that whenever there was a theft or fire they were always the first suspects. Their alibis usually lacked credibility and they often ended up being blamed for what they didn't do. When that was the case, they got very angry with the people who had framed them, and added their names to their long revenge list. Pretty soon half the town was on that list. Sen and Mo Gong took their time getting their revenge—little things here and there, like a chicken missing or a plot of vegetables ruined. They never left any evidence behind. It was their way of venting their feelings of being constantly maligned.

Siang became their friend by default. He was a good-looking fourteen-year-old from a wealthy family. His grandfather was an old revolutionary who had helped the Communist army occupy Putien and now received a big salary for doing nothing. He had used some of that money to build a huge three-storied home. Siang's mother was a nurse in a nearby hospital, and his father was a cadre in charge of a shoe factory.

Siang hated school and loved gambling. One year he lost so much money to Sen and Mo Gong that they were going to make him pay them back by stripping off his expensive clothes. He had begged for mercy and agreed to pay back the debt by buying them cigarettes for the next year. They became really good friends when Siang got kicked out by his parents and Mo Gong took him in. They slept in the same bed for a week before Siang got enough money to buy a ticket to go to Fuzhou to his grand-aunt, who was the president of the women's federation in the province of Fujian.

That left Yi, a short fifteen-year-old, who had become a carpenter at the age of twelve. He had goldfish eyes and bow legs. His parents had died young, and his grandpa had sent him away to be an apprentice at the age of ten. Yi said the first thing he learned from his carpenter master was how to slice his tobacco leaves and roll them into perfect rolls.

Another early carpentry lesson taught Yi how to chat nonstop while working, because it made one forget about the boredom and entertained others at the same time.

Then Yi's master died suddenly and Yi was forced to leave his apprenticeship two years ahead of time. His grandpa brought him home and set up a shop for him at the back of the street; he had been in business ever since.

He smoked bitter tobacco, drank strong tea constantly, and could go on chatting for hours without boring himself. He made all sorts of furniture for neighbors. But he was, after all, still a young boy, and his heart was out there on the street. Sen and Mo Gong often went to Yi's shop to swipe tobacco leaves when cash was low and the urge to smoke was clawing at them. In return, they had to keep the lonely carpenter company while he worked and endure listening to the same topics Yi had covered a hundred times before. But it wasn't a bad deal, really. When they were on the run from their parents or the law, Yi's humble workshop offered all they needed. It was out of the way in a back alley; tobacco leaves hung drying from the ceiling, liquor was kept nearby in Yi's toolbox, and food came from Grandpa's kitchen. They could even sleep on a worn blanket on the soft sawdust. On occasion, the shop was used as a gambling den. Yi spent more and more time with the gang and became a part-time carpenter and a full-time street kid.

Friendship endured.

Before I went back to school, I became an inseparable part of the now five-member gang. When school began, the group hung around the marketplace, harassed a few merchants, and bought candy and cigarettes. Then they climbed over the low wall at the back of my school and whistled to signal their arrival. As soon as the bell rang, I ran to the designated spot, where they lifted me up and threatened to toss me in the pond. Jumping back over the low wall, we lit cigarettes and made our plans for the day.

In school, I became sunnier and more confident. The results of last semester's countywide examination showed I was the best student in fourth grade, putting group one and La Shan's cronies to shame. In the hallways, the group one children still gave me dirty looks.

Once, when I passed the son of the party chief, he said, "Grades mean nothing. You are still a landlord's son." Then he laughed, showing his teeth like a vicious animal.

My teacher, Mr. Lan, took me aside and told me the same thing.

"Don't let your good grades get to you." It soon dawned on me that it was a sin to have scored so high and to have focused attention on myself. Now, in addition to the usual scorn, there was jealousy. I could do nothing right. But it no longer bothered me as much. When classes were over, I would see my friends again and would forget all about school. I no longer stayed up nights, plotting and scheming. Han, Quei, and Wang were still hateful, but now they were only small annoyances, little buzzing flies.

SEVEN

造

In the early seventies, Ping-Pong became the rage of the country because Zhuan Zhe Don had won the World Cup championship for China. In PE class, instead of the regular running and jumping in the dirt field, we would sit in the classroom and listen to the live radio report of the World Cup match in progress. With each score gained by a Chinese player against a Western player, we pounded our tables and cheered. When the games were over, we all sang, "The eastern winds blow and the drums of war echo. In today's world, who is afraid of whom? We are not afraid of the Russian and American imperialists. It is they who are afraid of us." The success of this Ping-Pong diplomacy made us swell like hot-air balloons. We were finally winning something in the international arena.

The school had a carpenter build two Ping-Pong tables. A stone slab served as a third table. During break, hundreds of kids crowded around the three tables and took turns playing. We played a three-point game.

Good players could stay in a game for a long time. Bad players were thrown out as quickly as they came. I became so involved that even after school I practiced at home. Gradually, I turned into one of the better Ping-Pong players on campus.

One weekend we heard that there was a new movie being shown twenty miles away from Yellow Stone in the capital city of Putien. That was a whopping distance of hills and valleys, especially if you had to wheel yourself around. The young tractor driver of our commune had seen it on one of his trips carrying fuel to the big city. A small crowd gathered around as he told everyone about how good it was. When he came to the description of the leading lady, he stopped, looked into our faces as if to prepare us for a shocker, then slowly made a few curves in the air with his hands and whistled.

"Is she that beautiful?" someone whispered.

The driver nodded. "Simply beyond words. Go see it." We were sold.

Sen took out his old bike, splashed it down with water, and sent a little boy to call me at home, respectfully keeping a distance from my strict mom.

"Your friends sent the messenger to call you," Mom said. He had apparently spilled our plans. "Be careful when you are in Putien. There is a lot of traffic there." To my surprise and delight, Mom gave me half a yuan for the trip.

Sen's bike was a museum piece. It rattled in places where it shouldn't have and was mute where it should have made noise. It was, nonetheless, mounted with a long backseat.

There were five of us; we rode that bike the acrobatic way. One pedaled, two straddled the backseat, and one sat sideways on the handlebars, barely giving the pedaler room to see. The fifth passenger ran behind and helped push the heavy load uphill. Every two miles we changed seating arrangements so that both runner and pedaler would get a rest. It was pathetic to see the old bike groaning under all that weight, slogging through the rough, muddy road with almost flat tires.

It took us a good three hours to reach Putien. We were covered with sweat and a layer of sand when we dismounted at the bridge, which looked like the entrance to the ancient city, and walked the rest of the way. Had a cop seen us, he would have thrown us off the bike for riding so dangerously in heavy traffic. He might even have taken the bike away, since Sen had never gotten a license for it.

Soon we were in front of the county's largest movie theater, pride and excitement gripping our hearts. We stared at the tall iron fences, the thick columns, and the fashionably dressed young people wearing their long, greasy hair ducktail style and sporting skintight bell-bottom trousers.

The girls wore colorful nylon skirts that flew above their creamy white knees as the sea wind whirled over the dusty ground. Since most women in China usually wore standard blue pants just like the men, this was a rare sight.

"Mo Gong is a little lost for words here," said Siang, the known cosmopolitan who had traveled far and often. He hit Mo Gong's head with the side of his hand.

"Tell us who these angels are, Siang," he said with his eyes glued to a particularly tall and leggy girl.

Siang took a long draw on his cigarette, narrowed his eyes like an old sailor, and said, "Those are the children of

Chinese families who came back after they were kicked out from places like the Philippines, Malaysia, and Indonesia when those places turned against the Chinese. Those foreign countries were all anti-China. Can you imagine?

"Now they live on a farm especially set aside for them by the government with a special supply store. They're rich people, with rich relatives back in their home countries who send them money monthly. A postman covering that area said that at the New Year he had to carry money to the farm in large canvas sacks." The five of us stood there admiring the youthful crowd as they rode around on fancy scooters, their girlfriends holding on to their waists. It didn't seem too bad a fate.

By the time we got to the theater, it was filled with smoke and the hallways were packed with people holding standing-room tickets. Kids hung from the windows trying to get a better view. On the platform stood a wide screen, with loudspeakers on either side. There were even children sitting behind the screen, looking up. They were going to watch the movie in reverse. We had to push and shove to get other viewers off our seats in the last row against the wall.

The place smelled like sweat and felt like an oven, but it was well worth all the trouble we'd been through to get there. The plot of the movie was run-of-the-mill Cultural Revolution stuff. The story took place in a seaside village. A landlord was plotting against the local Communist party, whose leader was the gorgeous goddess of curvy contours. In the end, the landlord was trashed and the good guys won.

Throughout the movie, I could hear Mo Gong and Sen ooh and ah with each close-up of the star. Siang was so drawn into the plot and carried away by the beautiful goddess that he forgot to smoke and almost burned his fingers.

We got home at nine in the evening, hungry and tired. Mom had cooked a pot of delicious noodles with vegetables and had kept it warm for me. With her approval, I took it to Yi's workshop and shared it with my buddies. First there was surprise that my mom had allowed me to do this; then there was a fight among my hungry friends to scoop up portions into their bowls. We slurped those long noodles silently. When we put down our chopsticks, full and relaxed, a warm feeling of being together like a family swept over us. We celebrated the good time with loud and long burps, laughing until our stomachs hurt.

Though we sat in a humble mud hut with a flickering kerosene light, it felt as if we had the whole world within our hearts.

EIGHT

"Open your schoolbag," Teacher Lan demanded.

"Why, Teacher? There are only books in it," I protested, sensing the eyes of Han, Quei, Wang, and the rest of the class searing into my back like the hot summer sun.

"Someone saw you smoking outside school," Teacher Lan said. "I think you've got cigarettes in your bag." I held on to my bag and shot a long, cold stare at Han, who sat with his feet on his desk, smiling acknowledgment. His cronies flanked him, grinning and showing their unbrushed teeth.

Teacher Lan snatched the bag from my hand. At the bottom lay an unopened pack of Flying Horse. I'd used the half yuan Mom had given me to buy them from Liang, the cigarette merchant, on my way to school. I had planned to share them with my friends over a good story at Yi's workshop.

"What is this?" Teacher Lan waved the pack in front of the whole class. "I helped you come back to school and make all that progress and now you want to throw away everything you have achieved. You are very stupid. You do not realize how people around here think of you. Some of them still want to throw you out of school. You just gave them good reason, and to tell you the truth, I am beginning to see their point.

"Those hoodlums will drag you down to the bottom again, even lower. Do you realize that? To the bottom." He threw the cigarettes on the floor, spat on them, and stomped them with his feet until they were totally crushed.

I had never seen the mellow, awkward Mr. Lan so forceful or so angry before, and I was shocked. He knew everything about my friends and me. I felt torn with pain at having our wonderful friendship trashed in front of my classmates and enemies. My head was becoming numb and my temples throbbed, but this time, instead of the old fear, I felt anger, anger at my enemies, who still picked on me at every opportunity, whose mission in life seemed to be my complete destruction.

They were ignorant of the beautiful, honest friendship those "hoodlums" offered me and would never be able to fathom the depth of our devotion to each other. Nor could Teacher Lan. He did not know how terrible school had been for me for so many years. I wanted to yell back at him and make him understand, but he had gone back to his podium, opened his book. Class had begun.

As my fury receded into a trickle of dull pain, I tried to digest what Teacher Lan had tried to tell me. There were people out there who were still trying to get me. Why didn't they leave me alone and let me just be like the rest of the kids? Who were they?

NINE

In the middle of the semester, a young teacher named Sing organized the yearly elementary school Ping-Pong match for the purpose of qualifying for the commune and eventually the county championship event. He was a decent guy with a head of salt-and-pepper hair.

I had always admired him for his many talents—calligraphy, basketball, writing, and he could play all kinds of musical instruments.

Each time he passed me, he greeted me readily. In fact, he was the only teacher who joked with me. One afternoon he came to my class and sat next to me with his arm over my shoulder. "How would you like to participate in the school championship match? I know you're pretty good."

"I'm not sure my political background would allow me to do so," I said uncertainly.

"I'll take care of it. You just make sure to be there for the game."

"Okay." My heart leapt with joy.

As far as Ping-Pong was concerned, there was only one other boy who played as well as I. If I wasn't there to challenge him, he would take the title, hands down.

That evening, I borrowed my brother's paddle and played three games in the match at the school cafeteria, a temporary game room. I spun and struck. Within two hours, I had defeated all the other players. The next night, with Sen, Siang, Mo Gong, and Yi watching from the windows, I beat my enemy, Han, and another opponent to become the champion for our commune. When the results were announced the next day at the morning exercise break, the whole school turned and looked at me. After so many years, I felt once again as though I belonged there. Proudly I waved my hands and bowed my head to their cheers.

The gratitude I felt for Teacher Sing was beyond words.

"We'd like to hold a swearing-in ceremony among us five at Mo Gong's tomorrow," Sen said one day. "What do you think?"

"You mean sort of like in ancient times, when the outlaws cut their fingers and let the blood drip into their wine and drank it together to become sworn brothers?" I asked excitedly.

"That's it," Sen said.

"And say something like, 'can't be born on the same day, but would like to die at the same moment.'" Mo Gong quoted a phrase from a well-known classic about a bunch of outlaws hiding deep in the mountains, who became sworn brothers and fought the establishment.

"I'm in," I said. "What do we need to do?"

"Prepare a banquet with some hard liquor."

The next day I went to Mo Gong's house, a two-story place that was totally empty since his parents had taken off again to sell shoes in another county. Siang had bought two lively young ducks from the market with my five yuan, and brought three pounds of pork from home. Yi came up with some vegetables and the noodles, and Sen ventured back home and had us sit under his kitchen window while he passed out some much-needed lard. We all pitched in to buy the liquor and cigarettes.

During his apprenticeship days, Yi had learned to cook. He was the only one who knew anything about it. I had resumed my usual job of washing the vegetables, picking over scallions and cutting them to match the specifications of the chef. Mo Gong chased the ducks in the backyard, causing the dirt and dust to fly, and Siang sharpened a knife, ready to behead them.

"Da, I want you to write some rules for us to go by," Sen said, squatting next to me.

"Let me think about it," I said.

When the food was finally brought to the table, along with chopsticks, spoons, and plates, we couldn't help shaking our heads in surprise. The two ducks, well simmered with garlic, ginger, wine, and Yi's secret soy sauce recipe, lay on a large plate with their skinny heads on one side. Next to them sat a deep pot with steaming pork shoulders, succulent and juicy. A king's feast was about to begin, and our stomachs growled in anticipation.

It seemed more like a normal, happy family meal than a swearing-in ceremony for a bunch of self-proclaimed outlaws. What civilization had done to us since the time of the kings and dynasties! We sat in order of seniority—Sen, Mo Gong, Yi, Siang, and me—clockwise around a circular wooden table. Sen opened the first bottle of liquor, a locally brewed rice wine that gave out a pungent fragrance of grain, and poured us each a tall glassful.

Wearing a serious look in those famous cold eyes, Sen declaimed, "Fate has brought us together. From now on we are brothers, not by blood, but by spirit."

"What happened to our swearing and all?" Mo Gong asked.

"That was the ancient thing. There's no need for slitting open our fingers," Sen said. "But I asked Da to write out a few rules that we all should live by faithfully."

"What happens if one of us doesn't follow the rules?"

"Here." Sen pounded his big fist on the table. "I'll take care of it."

"What if it's you?"

"The second-in-command would take over and have me punished the same way. Okay, what's the rules, Da?" Sen asked.

I took out a piece of paper and read solemnly: " 'No betrayal. No better friends outside than us. We suffer together, enjoy together. No jealousy. And we are all equal.' "

"Does everyone agree?" Sen glanced at each of us intently. We nodded.

"You all meant it, didn't you?" Sen shouted like an older brother.

We nodded again.

"This is serious. Anyone who can't live up to these rules, leave this place now," he shouted. "I don't want traitors in here."

The drama seemed to work. Everyone was quiet and thoughtful. For the first time, we all realized that it wasn't just food, drinks, smoking, and having fun together. It was more than that now. We were bound by rules. The moment filled me with strength, courage, and emotion. I felt I had grown a few inches.

"Now, bottoms up," Sen said, casting a long look at me in particular. "Da, you gotta do it."

"But I've never had anything this strong before," I protested. "Can I just have a few sips first?"

"This isn't strong—see?" Sen poured the whole thing down his throat. His face suddenly twisted into a fierce grimace. Then he turned red down to his neck. He opened his mouth as wide as he possibly could and waggled his tongue, fanning his mouth, wildly gasping for air.

After a long pause, when the liquor apparently had settled, Sen said, "See, I did it." His voice was raspy like sandpaper. We covered our mouths, trying not to laugh.

Then everyone did the same thing, clockwise.

When my turn came, I pinched my nose, closed my eyes, and downed the contents of the tall glass. As I had expected, it burned all the way to wherever it went inside my body. I could picture the flow of liquor, a stream of hot liquid steel, burning every inch of me. The miracle of pure alcohol. I instantly felt dizzy.

"How does it feel? Here, have some soup," Sen said, holding the spoon to my mouth. Yi and Mo Gong supported me, and Siang stuck a piece of duck inside my mouth to dispel the bad taste.

"Like fire." I coughed a few times, swallowed the soup, and chewed on the duck. My head was throbbing, and things began dancing around me. The whole house seemed to be moving in circles.

"Now, brothers," Sen said, "it's time to eat."

They dug into the duck. I went for a cigarette.

"Don't smoke now, it'll be like oil on fire, on top of liquor," I heard the wise voice of Yi say. But I lit one nonetheless. It felt heavenly.

For the rest of the banquet, I sat there dazed, watching the others laugh, chat, joke, drink, and smoke. They saved some food for me before we all went to sleep for the rest of the day.

When I awoke in darkness, my head ached as if a brick had hit it, throbbing with waves of pain each time I turned it. I struck a match and lit a candle and saw my newly sworn brothers snoring like a litter of puppies, huddled in one another's warmth. Sen was drooling on Yi's face and Siang was holding an empty bottle, his legs over Mo Gong's shoulder. I felt hungry and bet my friends would feel the same way. So I warmed up each dish and cleaned up the place, while putting on a kettle of fresh green tea to brew. Then I woke them up; they blinked like it was murder to be woken at this hour.

"Let's eat. Aren't you hungry?" They nodded, scratching their heads and yawning.

"First, hot tea to wake you all up, brothers!" I smiled as I served the steaming tea.

"Ah! I feel a heck of a lot better now with the tea, Da," Sen said. "Thanks. I'm sorry the liquor knocked you out like that. I didn't know it was strong enough to catch fire off the match. We all got knocked out."

"It was so strong my mouth still feels like rubber, and the food tastes like an old rag," Siang said.

We couldn't help laughing at ourselves. But laughter

wasn't the best thing at this moment. Each movement multiplied the pain attacking our heads and necks.

"I think they put fire powder in the liquor. It was a fake, Sen." More laughter. More pain.

By this time my dad had become quite an acupuncturist. Before Grandpa died, he had had a minor stroke, and Dad, unable to afford an acupuncturist for him, would study books on the ancient art, staying up late every night, sometimes even taking the old classics on Chinese herbal medicine to bed with him. After Grandpa died, Dad began offering free services to close friends and neighbors. Soon his reputation spread. He began to see patients in our home and sometimes even made house calls.

Under Dad's care, a few patients who had been paralyzed regained their ability to go to the bathroom and eat on their own. As his renown spread, a truck often drove him to treat patients in remote towns. Dad was shy about charging a fee, which would have made him an illegal practitioner. But people brought grain, rice, bananas, fish, shrimp, and all manner of food to repay him for his services. One of the patients even secured a temporary job at the county's canned food factory for one of my sisters.

Dad was a happier person. Even though he still had to work at a few more labor camps, he was treated differently. At one camp near the Ching Mountain, Mon Hai, a burly man with an unsightly birthmark over his right eye, was the supervising cadre. One evening he sent for Dad to be brought to his cabin. Much to my father's surprise, the cadre offered him a cigarette. Dad bowed humbly. Normally, the campers summoned to Mon Hai's cabin were there to be lectured or humiliated until midnight.

"I need a favor from you," Mon Hai said in an unusually low voice, after first closing his door and window.

"Anything, sir, I am here to be reformed."

"No, no, no, please sit down. I wanted you here for a different matter—shall I say, a private matter." The Communist smiled, revealing his gold-capped front teeth. "My dad fell last night and had a stroke. He is still in a coma and the doctor says he is paralyzed."

"I am sorry to hear that."

"You know what the doctor also said?" Mon Hai lit a cigarette for my father.

"What did he say?"

"That you are the only one in this area who could cure him."

"No, no, I'm an amateur. It is purely a hobby, that's all. I did try treatments on my own now-dead father, but I would not call myself a doctor or anything like that. You should really seek other help," my father mumbled nervously.

"Are you saying no to me?"

"I'm not, cadre. You don't understand," Dad said.

"Then what is it?" Mon Hai asked. "Money? That's no problem. My brother is the head of a fertilizer factory and he has loads of money."

"No, it is not money." Dad shook his head.

"I know what it is. You are afraid."

Dad remained silent.

"It's totally understandable. I would be also if I were you, but please don't be. Just try to treat me as if I'm one of your regular patients."

Yeah, right. Dad could still feel the pain inflicted on his back where Mon Hai had kicked him for slowing down at another campsite. Mon Hai's father sounded as if he was in critical condition, and if anything happened to him, Dad would be blamed.

"I really wouldn't feel comfortable, cadre."

"Look at me, Doctor, I also have a heart." The cadre pulled open his shirt for emphasis. "I apologize for what I have done to you."

"No, no. There is no need for that."

"I shouldn't have kicked you." The man's eyes turned misty. "I'm sorry. I will make it up to you."

Dad was quiet, watching this bear of a man tearing his guts out.

"Even if I agree to take a look, I wouldn't be able to do so. We are not allowed to leave the campsite."

"I'll take care of that."

Dad was told to stay in his cabin the next morning while the rest of the campers rolled out of their beds and headed for the chilly mountain to dig some more hills and fill some more valleys. At nine o'clock, a biker came by and picked Dad up, carrying him to Mon Hai's house a few miles away.

It turned out to be a light stroke. Mon Hai's old man was only sixty-five and in good health. It took Dad about two months to bring him back to where he could walk with only a slight limp.

At the reform camp, Dad hardly had to touch his farming tools. He had been ordered to stay behind and write confessions, but in fact all he did was read his medical books and be taken to see the patient every day. He was allowed to come home for dinner after dark three times a week. The rest of the time he spent at the cadre's cabin, where Mon Hai would do his drinking and pour out his admiration for Dad. It was there that Dad learned that the good food, liquor, and cigarettes that Mon Hai shared with him all came from the campers, who bribed Mon Hai for lighter work and a guarantee that they would avoid punishment. In one of his drunken states, Mon Hai even revealed that he had occasionally slept with the young wife of a newly branded counterrevolutionary, a camper under his supervision. He further admitted that he slept with the wife at her request because she wanted to ensure that the poor young man would live to see his infant son.

Dad itched to inflict some pain on that son of a whore and offered Mon Hai the use of his needles to cure his drinking addiction, but he refused.

One day Mon Hai was suddenly rushed back from the work site where he spent an hour a week on inspection. Two strong young men took turns carrying him on their backs.

"Chen, come here," they said to my father. "Mon Hai was hurt." A rock had rolled down the side of the hill and landed on his waist, bruising him badly before bouncing off into a ditch.

"Doctor, I think I could use some of those needles you got there," Mon said, looking up in pain from his bed.

"I think so too," Dad replied.

During the following weeks, Dad gave Mon Hai double the number of treatments necessary. He chose longer, thicker needles and spun them harder, telling Mon that he would improve faster that way. Mon Hai would shake with fear as he watched Dad slowly prepare the needles, wiping them on an alcohol pad. He would squirm in anticipation of the pain until the needles were actually inserted under the skin; then his hysterical and terrifying screams could be heard for miles around.

Before each session Mon Hai begged for more, and during every session he cursed and rolled in agony. After each of my father's visits, he would shed tears of gratitude. His pain soon disappeared, and Gang Chen openly became known around camp as the Doc.

Dad was discharged from labor camp early that year and received a glorious report on how his anti-Communist way of thinking had improved. The report was signed in big letters by the now-healthy Mon Hai, who ironically was selected by the people of Yellow Stone as an outstanding member of the Communist party. His picture appeared on a wall outside the commune headquarters, only to be washed off a week later by a cold winter rain.

TEN

Zhang Tie Shan, an army recruit from north China, wrote a big zero on his college exam paper accompanied by the following words: "To make revolution, one need not answer above questions."

Instantly he became a hero throughout China, epitomizing the true spirit of the Cultural Revolution. School became chaos. Everyone ran around mindlessly, doing nothing. Teachers could do almost nothing to remedy the situation for fear of being branded stinking intellectuals or counter-revolutionaries.

Our fifth-grade classes were made up of three categories: labor, politics, and self-study. We dug up the playground and turned it into vegetable plots so that young kids could labor under the scorching sun and have empty but healthy minds. We had to bring all the necessary tools to water, weed, and harvest the vegetables, then sell our crop back to the teachers at a discount, using the money to buy more seeds and plant more vegetables.

In the political science classes, teachers read the newspaper to the students. When we were left to study on our own, the chairs became hurdles. We jumped them and counted the minutes until it was time to go home.

Every day after class, Dad read me classics that we had buried under the pigsty. In the mornings I learned to play the bamboo flute. Dad said a real scholar should know poetry, chess, calligraphy, and music.

The flute was the cheapest thing to study. Dad bought me one from the local market. At sunrise every morning, I got up, pulled the skinny bamboo flute from under my pillow, and tiptoed to the backyard and down the steps that led to the Dong Jing River. I'd wash my face with the refreshing water and postpone my morning bowel movement because it gave me more power as I blew the flute. Each day, I broke the silence of the morning in Yellow Stone, standing by the river and playing innocent folk melodies. The sound bounced off the water, crossed the vast green fields, and ended in a lingering echo as it reached the mountains on the horizon. The occasional mooing from the buffalo told me that at least someone was listening.

One day, Dad came back from a month's stay at a labor camp and rushed to the backyard where I was practicing.

"Son, you play beautifully now," he said, surprised. He gathered me into his arms and roughed me up excitedly. "I hardly believed my ears as I walked along the fields. I could hear you a mile away from here."

"Dad, do you really like it?" I asked.

"Like it? I love it. I think with a little tuning here and

there, you're ready to perform in an amateur troupe some-where and eventually graduate to a professional one."

"Do you want me to be a professional?"

"Well, school is doing nothing now, not with that Zhang-something guy in fashion. It's wonderful that you have a skill. You have an edge over others."

From then on I practiced even harder—much to the an-noyance of my family—and I began to hang around the re-hearsal hall of our commune's performing group. In the evenings, I would invite my friends to come with me to the rehearsals at the commune. They went and clung to the windows for a glimpse of the young and pretty actresses and laughed their heads off when those pretty things teased each other and giggled in singsong voices.

There was an outstanding, arrogant flutist in the troupe from Putien City who was paid to be the music director of the orchestra. He was a woodwind expert and could even play the French horn. Every morning he demanded at least five precious eggs. For lunch, half a chicken. And for dinner, lots of pork and another five eggs. He said playing the French horn and the flute used up all his energy and he needed the nutrients. Hungry kids actually trooped by to sniff his French horn, which smelled like eggs.

I copied his techniques and replayed the music by ear. At Yi's, my friends would listen to my flute and smoke in silence.

As my interest in music grew, I became fascinated with the violin.

The first time I heard one, I was picking grains of rice from the muddy rice fields under a summer sun. The commune had set up a crackling loudspeaker at the edge of the fields and played a simple violin solo through it. The music was supposed to cheer the farmers, and I fell head over heels in love with it. It was sensuous and tender and caressed my soul in a way that no instrument had done before. I stood there holding the dripping rice, lost in the beauty of the music.

"Go to work," a farmer's voice behind me urged. She was the opposite of what a violin was. I bent down again and went on working, the melody resonating deep in my soul.

I wanted to learn that instrument, but how?

Once again, Dad came through like a champ. This time he contacted a young man named Soong, originally from the city of Putien. He was the son of a Christian dentist who had died in jail, and he had taken over his father's old practice. The family had been labeled counterrevolutionaries because of their dogged belief in God and had been sent to live in exile in Heng Tang, a tiny village near Yellow Stone.

Dad had heard of Soong on one of his visits to a patient who was a neighbor of Soong's and who had complained often about the strange, foreign music the young man played at night.

Having met with Soong, Dad reported that the young man had readily agreed to teach me the basics if I was willing to walk there every day during the summer vacation.

The fifth grade finished without the expected finals and report cards. Everyone graduated. But whether I was going to high school remained a mystery. Politics was in; grades were out. My fate stood undecided, wavering in the wind like a blade of grass along the Dong Jing River.

Heng Tang was nestled at the foot of Hu Gong Mountain. When the sky was overcast, the village floated like a mirage among the clouds. When it rained, it totally disappeared. During the summer, it was hidden under the thick foliage of persimmon trees, but in spring the village blossomed like a wild garden.

I finally arrived at Mr. Soong's dental office, in an old temple at the edge of the village.

"Da, right?" Soong greeted me warmly, taking off his surgical mask.

He had just finished with a teary-eyed young boy who was being comforted by his mom.

"Mr. Soong. How did you know it was me?"

"The violin." He smiled and revealed the whitest teeth I had ever seen. I supposed it came with the business.

I smiled back, hiding my teeth, regretting not having brushed them again before coming. I studied him as he washed his hands and hung up his white coat. He was in his twenties, fair-skinned and good-looking, with long hair that touched his collar. He wore a pair of tight bell-bottom trousers and a silk shirt. A city dude to the bone.

"A barefooted violinist?" he said, smiling at me. "Let's see what you've got there."

I took out the violin and he plucked a few notes on it, adjusted the pegs, redid the bridge, tightened the bow, then cradled it between his neck and shoulder. He closed his eyes and a soothing melody flowed out of my instrument. His fingers ran quickly along the strings, up and down, and the bow jumped, making curt sounds. I was amazed at his skill and was falling in love with the music when he stopped suddenly.

"You got a great violin here." He put it down carefully. "Smoke?" I shook my head.

"Want to be an artist?" I nodded, not knowing where he was heading.

"Then take one." He threw me a filtered cigarette and lit it for me with a lighter. I puffed on it and inhaled deeply. "I'm no teacher. Don't call me *Teacher* or anything, but I could use a friend like you." He looked out his small window, then at a pile of dentures lying on his messy desk. "It's boring here. In fact, if you want to be a dentist, I can teach you that as well. I have plenty of time on my hands and all these teeth need to be filed to fit into patients' mouths."

"I'll do the violin first," I replied, "but I can help with your work during my break."

"No need, I was joking."

It didn't take me long to like him.

The next few days I spent walking around his office, holding my violin between my shoulder and neck and practicing bowing. It was a painful experience that made my neck swell and left my shoulder raw, but he kept saying I was making progress. He showed me pictures of stone busts of Beethoven and Mozart and told me stories about them, amazing stories.

I practiced constantly and was making fast progress, which Mom and Dad noticed with considerable pride. To thank Soong, Mom would sometimes ask me to bring fruit and meat to him, and Dad sent him cartons of cigarettes and liquor, gifts given him by his acupuncture patients. Soong would cook the food I brought and ask me to stay for dinner, then send me home on his bike in the evening. Sometimes, when his mother was visiting his brothers, I'd bring a lot of food and stay over for the weekend. There would be no violin lessons or any other music during those times. We would go hunting.

Near the end of the summer, Soong said, "Da, there isn't much I can teach you anymore. From here on, you have to practice and just figure it out for yourself. Besides, school is starting soon, right?"

"I'm not sure I'm going to high school."

"What do you mean? Of course you're going. You're so young."

"I haven't got my notice yet. Others already did." I hung my head.

"Come on, young fellow. Don't feel bad; you could always come to learn dentistry with me. Kids are learning nothing in school now anyway." He smiled. "But I want you to come and visit me on weekends and I'll take you to Putien to meet some of the coolest young musicians in the city."

"I promise."

Finally I was issued a notice stating that after careful consideration by the commune education board, I would not be given the opportunity to pursue my schooling any further. Neither was I allowed to do so at other schools in another commune.

No reason given. No reason needed.

A patient of Dad's secretly told us that the board's reason was simple. My ancestors and family had had enough education; it was time we made do without more.

I felt sad and isolated again. Everyone in my school went on to high school, even the worst of the students. I couldn't go because my dad had gone to college, as had my grandpa. What kind of reasoning was that? Why did I have to carry the burden of my parents' generation?

Mom prayed day and night, promising three chickens and four piglets to Buddha if any high school accepted me. I promised a thousand kowtows on my own. And then good news came in an unusual way. Dad's regular guest, the sugar-cane farmer, casually mentioned that he had delivered some high-quality fresh canes to the high school last night because the almighty principal's aging father had just had a stroke. The only thing he could eat was juice squeezed from the fresh sugarcane. The principal was upset and restless and didn't know what to do.

That evening at dinner, a young high school teacher came hurriedly to our house and wanted to meet Dad privately. Dad took him into our back room. Five minutes later, Dad emerged and said he was going to the see the principal's father right away because the patient was still in critical condition.

He came back late. The news was good. I would be in the fourth group in grade one of junior high a month later. The delay was due to the specific order from the commune that I was not to be admitted under any condition. They would sneak me in after all the hubbub died down. I thanked Dad and then crawled quietly to the attic, got on my knees, and kowtowed a whopping thousand and five times. Five extra were done to make up for any possible miscalculation in the hasty up-and-down motions.

ELEVEN

造

"You're the guy who plays the violin, I heard."

"Yeah, what do you want?" I looked up from a stack of new textbooks to see a well-dressed fellow sauntering up to me. His clothes were neatly layered from the inside out. He wore shoes and socks with brightly colored patterns, a rarity among Yellow Stone boys. He was flanked by a couple of shorter fellows with toothy grins.

"Nothing, nothing, just a casual visit." He stuck out his hand. As the sleeve rode up, a gold watch glistened in the morning sun that filtered through the window of our classroom. "Name is I-Fei. Do you care for a cigarette during the break?"

He became my best friend in class. His pomposity came from his family's background. His father was the mayor of Han Jian, the second largest town in Putien. His mother was the president of the women's federation at a government dry goods manufacturing factory. Both were seasoned Communist cadres. His parents had become too caught up with their lives and had deposited him at his aunt's, thus making him a big fish in a small pond. He lived on a fabulous monthly stipend and rode a brand-new bicycle to school once in a while, just to show it off to the girls. The teachers tolerated him because his mother controlled the supply of sugar and cooking oil in the county. She was all sugar and oil. Poorly paid, some teachers often could be seen begging I-Fei for oil and sugar coupons, which would allow them to buy those rare commodities, unobtainable on their pathetic rations.

I-Fei searched out interesting fellows in school and made alliances with them. Even the cool guys in senior high greeted him like an old pal. He dragged me around wherever he went and introduced me as his buddy. We were the same height and build; soon we were wearing the same hairstyle. I even asked Mom for socks to wear, a giant step for someone who had only operated in bare feet before.

By midterm, I was on the school Ping-Pong team and also in the school band. Three days a week I practiced Ping-Pong after school, and the rest of the week I played the flute and stumbled along on my violin, preparing for the rehearsal of a grand seven-act play directed by Mr. Ma, the high school drama teacher.

Schoolmates were amazed by my violin. They called it "the shoulder thing." There were always eager faces pasted at the windowpanes of the rehearsal hall. Now they had one more thing to look at besides the alluring faces of the school's stars.

Soon I was a recognizable face in a school of two thousand students.

"Did you hear that?" I-Fei asked me angrily one day as we walked into the rehearsal room.

"What?" I asked.

"There was a guy out there, bad-mouthing you, calling you a landlord's son, and this and that." I-Fei's face was burning.

"Who was it?"

"A skinny little rat from group one called Han or something. Aren't you going to do anything about it?" He put his hands on his waist.

"Listen, he was my old enemy from elementary school."

"And you let him run through you like that?"

"I'll take care of him later."

"Not later." He stared at me. "Now."

"I don't want to make a scene here."

"I'll make a scene. Let's go."

"Not now. You don't understand."

"I do understand. They used to pick on you, but not in here."

He marched me out of the room and we went toward a small crowd.

"You stay cool, okay," I-Fei said in a hushed voice, "and do as I say."

"What are you going to do?" The fear of getting kicked out of school washed over me again.

He didn't answer. I saw him walk straight to Han, who stopped laughing and turned to face I-Fei.

"You've been cursing me behind my back, you son of a whore," I-Fei shouted, spitting at Han and waving his fists.

"I wasn't talking about you," Han said. "I was talking about him."

He pointed at me.

"That's not true, I heard you do it." I-Fei moved in closer; his eyes were popping. He started to push Han. Han pushed back.

"Come on, Da," I-Fei yelled. "Now the rat confessed he has been cursing both of us. How dare you!" My blood rushed to my head. The old pain began to come back. I was shaking and trembling.

"Come on, Da!" Suddenly I turned fearless and hit Han right in the temple with my fist. Han stumbled back a few steps. I-Fei ducked down and swung his right foot against Han's unsteady legs. Han fell onto the dirt ground. A cheer went up among the crowd.

My legs flew and I started kicking him in his chest and groin. He screamed. I-Fei pinned his head down. Then I jumped on him and hit him till my arms were exhausted. We let go of him.

Han crawled to his feet like a dog hit by a truck and limped away, mud, sweat, and tears covering his face. I was in tears too.

"Why are you crying?" I-Fei asked, puzzled.

"Happy." I wiped my face. "Thanks."

"He would never dare look you in the face from now on."

That evening, Mr. Ma took us into his office and severely criticized us. I said it was my fault, I-Fei said it was his. Mr. Ma said if it were not for the upcoming dress rehearsal of the revolutionary drama, we would all be fired from the production. We tried to suppress our laughter as we left the office.

Our show was ready by the New Year. For that period, we had already gotten fifteen bookings, mainly from the small villages that made up the Yellow Stone commune. Our play was about how a female high school student, at first a bookworm, was helped by the Red Guards to join the revolutionary camp. She became a Red Guard and denounced her past affiliation with a counterrevolutionary, who was trying to corrupt her young mind with intellectual studies. The total cast was about fifty people, including teachers. It was not much of a play, but to a village where there might be a movie once a year, any form of entertainment was reason to celebrate, especially when it coincided with the New Year.

A few days before the New Year, we were invited to perform in the village of Ding Zhuan, where my distant cousin Wen Qui lived, and where I had hidden myself earlier. Now it was time for a happy reunion.

In the morning, the village sent tractors to pick us up. We sang all the way there, crowded into the back. When we arrived, small children chased us with interest. "The music men are here!" they shouted.

The band's job when we got to each destination was to hang all the curtains, layers of them, and set up all the props. Ding Zhuan had an outdoor dirt platform facing a large square. A few bamboo poles were erected at the four corners. I-Fei and I climbed up the poles and tied the curtains to them while others carried the heavy props to the back of the stage and passed the curtains to us. Teachers shouted at us as we rocked on the tip of the poles for fun. Then we helped the electricians set up the spotlights.

Out in the dirt yard, villagers had long since claimed their spots with their own chairs, camping out since the day before. These kids hadn't had such fun for a long time. At the village headquarters, where all of us would be staying for the night, a large kitchen was preparing a banquet for us.

"Three big fat pigs and lots of other food," the chief of the village said proudly. "You will have plenty to eat." He passed out cigarettes on a tray to everyone, including the students. Mr. Ma stared at us like a disapproving parent and snatched them all back.

That afternoon, I visited my cousin Wen Qui, bringing along my violin.

"Welcome, welcome. I didn't expect to see you." Wen looked a few years older and now had an unruly mustache. "All I knew was that you were in high school." He was beaming with joy. His wife patted my shoulders lovingly.

"I am in high school and I'm playing the violin now."

"Just like your dad. That's very good. Here, play something for us."

I played a simple melody and they listened quietly.

"I can see you are surviving well, on the school propaganda team and all. It makes me think of the old days, when you were hiding here," my cousin said sentimentally.

His wife's eyes were misty, but she smiled and held my hands in hers.

"How is school?"

"Well, no one is serious about school nowadays. That's why I'm doing this." I plucked a few notes and put the violin away.

"But it's difficult to make a living doing that, unless you're very talented."

I was quiet.

"It's fun, singing and dancing and lots of good food—and probably lots of smoking. I've done all that before." Wen Qui looked at his wife, who smiled back. "But you should try to study as much as possible in school."

"What's the use?"

"What's the use? Knowledge. Nobody can take that away from you. Times will change, then you'll be sorry," he said.

I stayed quiet. I had gone there expecting to talk about my exciting winter schedule with my favorite couple, discussing my music and friends.

He had just dumped a bucket of cold water on my head.

"He mentions this because we care for you," his wife added gently. "You're a really smart kid. Don't waste your talent."

"It's wonderful to have a hobby, but go back and study hard. You will thank me when you grow up," Wen added.

In the audience that evening, I didn't see Wen or his wife. As he had said, he had done it all and seen it all in his youth. I believed him, and I loved them both.

That night after the banquet, I-Fei and I took a walk along a dark dirt road.

"What are you going to do when you grow up?" I asked.

"Not sure yet," I-Fei said. "I could work for my mom and be an oil and sugar man. But Dad wants me to be a driver."

"Why?"

"You make the most money, only second to being a butcher."

Under-the-table money.

"How about going to college?"

"I don't want to be a stinking intellectual. I'm from a revolutionary family. What do you want to be?"

"A violin soloist, performing before thousands of fans in a great concert hall. I want to travel by plane, wear good suits and ties, and have female fans fainting at my feet."

I-Fei couldn't stop laughing. I hit his back with my fist and he stopped. But I agreed with him, it was a ridiculous dream.

"That I couldn't help you with," he said earnestly. "If you want to be a teacher or something, my dad might be able to help get you a job."

"I don't need your help. I'll study hard and make it on my own."

"Study? Are you crazy?"

I nodded.

He offered me a cigarette. For the first time, I refused.

"What's the matter with you?"

"Nothing. Just don't feel like one."

He lit one for himself. I took it out of his mouth and threw it away.

He tried to hit me but I was already a few steps beyond him. We ran back to the headquarters. All the way, I felt the eyes of Wen and his wife staring at me, smiling and hoping.

TWELVE

On the ninth day of the ninth month of 1976, Chairman Mao died like an ordinary man. Superstitious farmers said nine was the number of an emperor and heaven had intended that he die like an emperor. It could have been a coincidence, but the sun, covered by clouds, didn't shine over Yellow Stone for ten days following his death. Rumor had it that it was mourning the loss of a great leader, but Dad thought the sky was upset because Mao hadn't died earlier. But a leader, no matter how rotten, was almost a supernatural figure. Confucianism had taught people to be obedient to the emperor unconditionally. Mao's rule had reinforced such a tradition. For days after his death, people gathered in knots, in the fields, under the trees, whispering quietly and mysteriously as though a disaster were about to befall the whole nation.

Mom and Dad told me to be especially careful about what I said.

We, the enemies of Mao, should not appear to be gleeful about the news.

The leaders of the commune could thrash every one of us before the system changed. We could be easy targets for their wrath in mourning. There might be martial law, even civil war, Dad cautioned.

Even though my parents' generation hated him, I had embraced Chairman Mao in my own way. I didn't know any better. A cult mentality had already been forged in me. In my heart, there was no other leader who mattered as much, regardless of how good or bad he was. I had been told not to analyze him because he was wiser, no, the wisest. I was to follow him and love him with all my heart.

Leaders and cadres of Yellow Stone commune held long meetings, during which some were said to have cried until they collapsed. There was a sense that they had lived their golden days and that what might be ahead was totally unknown.

In the street, people wore black bands on their right arms. Day and night, the gloomy and weeping sounds of Mao's funeral music haunted every dusty corner of Yellow Stone, transmitted through temporary loudspeakers. It never stopped.

As though the rift between the Red families and the landlords' families were widened by the death of Mao, I was told by the school authorities not to attend the funeral ceremony. Landlords' families were not invited. I was saddened, humiliated, confused. I had thought I was slowly blending into the system after changing schools. Now they told me I couldn't go and mourn the most forbidding leader, the only leader, I knew. It hurt me deeply to be separated from such an event.

I wanted to say good-bye to him, the dead Chairman Mao, but I didn't even have a black armband.

One day sometime later, on my way home from school, I saw a large crowd gathered at the market square. A young man with a large brush was splashing characters on a white wall that read, DOWN WITH THE GANG OF FOUR! Who were the Gang of Four? I stood closer at the edge of the crowd, watching. The young man wrote the names one after another, to the total surprise of all.

Jiang Qing (formerly known as Madam Mao), Yiao, Zhang, and Wang.

It couldn't be. How could Mao's wife be down while Mao's bones were still warm? Mao's wife had been running the country since Mao had been sick. *Someone is taking over the government,* I thought with alarm. Maybe there would be a war, as Dad had said. I rushed home and breathlessly told Dad the news.

"Are you sure?" he asked. "They could throw you in jail if you spread untrue rumors."

I told him I hadn't made it up. He grabbed Mom and closed the door behind them. I could hear them whispering and laughing.

That evening the bikers, who spent their days carrying passengers back and forth from the city of Putien and Yellow Stone for thirty fen each trip, confirmed the breaking news. They said people were painting the names of the Gang of Four on the cement streets in Putien and then crossing them out. Some even made effigies and burned them. At nine o'clock that night, through a crackling radio system, there was a special announcement from the central government confirming the downfall of the Gang, which had consisted of some leading figures in Mao's cabinet.

On my way back from school one day, I saw a large crowd standing outside the house that belonged to the party chief of Yellow Stone commune. I could hear a boy sobbing amid the chatter. I stopped, jumped on a vegetable peddler's stool, and strained to see what was happening. Two cops were brushing glue on the front door of the house and pasting white paper over it. They were sealing the house, as they had done to those of the landlords and counterrevolutionaries just a few years ago. And the chief's son was wiping his eyes with his sleeves, standing obediently by a bicycle packed with his belongings.

I asked an old man standing next to me what was going on. He said they had gone to arrest the chief that day, only to find that he had escaped early in the morning, leaving his son behind. And now they were sealing his house and sending his son away to his grandpa, who lived in the mountains.

Well, I thought, *the chief, the formidable chief, is now a criminal fugitive and he has abandoned his son.* I still remembered that it was he who had spat at me in the school hallway and plotted with my teacher, La Shan, to kick me out of school in third grade. I didn't think he ever thought this would happen to him. I thought about La Shan, secretly hoping that he might end up being hunted like the party chief, with whom he had tried so hard to ingratiate himself.

Dad wasn't surprised to hear the news. He said that soon we would be able to do what others could do—like going to school and finding a job. I nodded in disbelief as Dad kept saying, "Son, you could be the lucky one."

In school, I was getting by with the help of others. I had become everything I was not in elementary school, popular with friends, with nobody picking on me. But teachers looked at me as if I didn't belong there. I was behind in all the subjects. They didn't try to help me. They generally left me alone, and I was forgotten. They thought I was the rotten type that they had to cut off, so they never inquired about my homework and never asked me questions in class. They knew I hadn't prepared for it. I was always with I-Fei, leaving early to rehearsals or coming back late from them. It was a wonderful feeling for a while, because now I had finally become what I had wished to be and could not be in elementary school. There were no enemies chasing me at every corner, concocting dirty tricks behind my back every day. I was respected and had a lot of friends, significant friends. I was my own master. I did not have to fear, worry, or fight. I felt safe and anchored.

But soon I was feeling empty about school. I used to love studying and had known the joy of being at the top of the class. I knew about basking in affirming smiles from the teachers, people my family had taught me to respect. Though I was having a good time, I felt as if I was violating something special.

In class, serious teachers began to talk about the possibility of restoring our country's college system. During the Cultural Revolution, all colleges either were closed, or they enrolled only a small number of students from politically correct families through a corrupt system of selection. The teachers would end their speeches by saying that even the musicians had to pass other tests to go to art school. They would cast a look my way.

The more they talked about college, the more I was determined that I wanted to be an artist, because I was doing so badly in school. I was sure I was beyond hope, academically speaking. I had to do something with my life.

One day that winter, Mo Gong ran breathlessly to our home and told me that our county's performing troupe was holding public auditions for actors and instrument players. I was so excited that the next day I-Fei and I rode his bike and headed for Putien so that I could sign up for the audition. During the next few days, Dad dug out some old music scores, traditional classics that had been banned for the past twenty years, and said, "The Red Guard music is over. Pick one of these for your audition." He understood my feelings and appreciated my passion for art. After all, it was he who had inspired me.

His friends had only to make the slightest demand and he would nudge me into playing a few songs on my violin, which his friends mysteriously called "the Western instrument." He would introduce the violin, explaining the relationship between the four strings, and show off the amazing range of the tiny instrument by plucking the strings with his fingers. Sometimes he would ask me to tag along on his occasional gigs playing classic Chinese folk music for weddings, which probably made me the first to render the thousand-year-old melodies on such an instrument. At those gigs, traditional instruments—gongs, drums, and flutes—usually drowned out my tiny violin.

Soong had warned me of the temptation to play everything on the violin. Being a purist, he had asked me how I could play that stupid traditional music on something on which so many magnificent masterpieces had been played. He said it would ruin my style, but I had ignored him. I wanted to make Dad happy.

Since the classic romantic plays were coming back into fashion as Dad had foretold, I concentrated on my flute, not the Western instrument, for the audition. For three days, I practiced only three short classical pieces while Dad listened and coached. On the day of my audition, my sister Si carried me on the bike to Putien at sunrise, where we waited in a long line of self-proclaimed artists, eating our packed breakfast of cold and dried yams.

My teeth kept clicking as the line began to move. I had to run to the smelly bathroom every five minutes for a two-second pee. Si saw how nervous I was and said that I was still very young and that if I failed this time, I could always try again. I thought about my friends and about I-Fei. If they had been here, they would have lit a good cigarette for me, kicked me in the butt, and tried to make me smile. I yearned for a cigarette, but the thought of having a coughing fit during the performance stopped the terrible urge.

When I heard my number called, my sister patted my back, and I walked slowly into the hall. It was an old, small theater. As I walked, my footsteps echoed. Before me sat six of the most prominent musical figures in our county.

Teacher Dong, a big fish stranded in a small town, was the only college graduate with a music major from Fuzhou Music Conservatory. He wore his glasses on the tip of his nose and looked at me without an ounce of interest in his drooping eyes. Ding, the famous Putien opera singer, was filing her nails. Flutist Min, the first flute of the county, was slumped low in his armchair. Drummer Jia was reading an old newspaper, and Director Liao, a bearded man, smoked a pipe, fighting the numbing boredom without much success.

I felt small and unworthy.

"What will you do?" Flutist Min asked. "Not another flutist again?"

I hoped he was joking.

" 'A Trip to Gu Su,' " I mumbled. My teeth were still chattering.

95

All I could think of was my sister's worried look as I left her, the fetid public bathroom, and the sagging eyes of the music teacher. I forced the first sound out of my old flute. The flute sounded as if it was crackling and getting dry, so I started again. It was a steep uphill ride. I couldn't breathe at all. My heart pounded like a rat in an iron cage.

From the corner of my eye, I saw an uncomfortable twitching of Flutist Min's nose. He must be so disgusted. I was sure I had ruined it with the first note. Gradually, I forced my eyes to close and tried to think of the peaceful Dong Jing River by which I had practiced every morning, the green fields that stretched beyond it, and the colors of the mountain at sunrise. Soon the desire to win started to churn within me. I remembered every twist and turn Dad had taught me during the last three days. When the final note had faded away, I opened my eyes to see that all the judges were making busy notes.

Flutist Min was the first to look up. He smiled at me and said, "Well done. It didn't start out right, but you handled the piece unusually well. Come here. Let me have a word with you."

I walked over to Min's chair.

"Here, let me tell you the truth about this audition. We have enough flutists already. Do you play any other instrument?"

"The violin."

"No good. We are going back to the old things now— you know, the sort of stuff banned by the Gang of Four. If you are serious about our troupe, try out as an actor. Have you acted before?"

"Not really."

"Go home and make up your mind about your career.

This is not just for amusement. You need to think and talk to your parents, put your heart into it. If you are still interested, I'll be happy to talk to you. But no instruments. We only need good actors who have the classic looks to perform all those classic plays. Got that?"

I thanked him and left the hall.

My sister was smiling at me, waiting. She said I did a good job. I told her about the conversation I had had with the flutist.

I was quiet during the ride back. I wasn't going to be an artist, nor a carpenter, nor a shoemaker. Definitely not a farmer. For a while I was lost. Time had changed everything for me, and I was always behind, it seemed, like chasing my own shadow. What had once been right wasn't right anymore. I wished I knew the future, while hoping that the past would not be repeated.

Dad said it would probably be a good time to start being serious about school. He had just heard from my aunt in Shanghai that her son was already preparing for the college entrance examinations that were open to all test-takers, regardless of age, race, or family background. People would be admitted solely on the basis of their scores.

He added that I was the only one in our family who was still in school and therefore able to benefit from such great news.

I went to sleep with a heavy heart. I kept thinking about the indifferent way the teachers treated me. I had been acting like a bad student.

No, I *was* a bad student. Now I was miles behind everyone. It was unfair. When I was a good student, winning honor for the elementary school with perfect marks, they hadn't needed high marks. Now, when they did want them, I was at the bottom.

Next day, I put away my music, wrapped up the small Beethoven bust that I had kept at my bedside, and stored it under my bed. I loosened the strings on my violin and locked its wooden box. Then I searched for all the textbooks I had long since stopped bringing to school. They were new, untouched, and covered with dust. I cleaned them and laid them neatly on the desk beside my bed. Slowly I leafed through the physics book. It was filled with strange symbols and new formulas, expressed in oddly shaped letters and filled with words I couldn't understand. It didn't look as if I could just close my eyes and sink my teeth into the subject. The only formula I recognized was H_2O. I shut the books with dismay and hopelessness. Time had deserted me, or, rather, I had deserted myself. The knife of regret cut deeply into my soul.

Finally, I opened my English book. On the first page I had drawn the face of my wheezing English teacher, with his dead eyes and stooped back. The sketch had really captured his spirit. I gave a small laugh and turned the page. It listed the twenty-six letters of the English alphabet.

I stood up, closed my bedroom door to make sure no one would hear me, and twisted my tongue and lips trying to pronounce each letter. I could only get as far as *F.* Next to the letter G I had drawn a chicken, because the Chinese word for chicken came closest to the sound of the English G. The letter *H* became *love paint.* For the rest, the symbols I had drawn and characters I had written next to them didn't help. It was another dead subject for me. I slammed the book closed and stared at my violin for a long time, until I drifted into a little nap.

"Hey, what's this?" I-Fei asked jokingly the following morning before class. "Is this a schoolbag, or are my eyes seeing things?"

"We have to do some studying," I said seriously.

"We have no time for this, Da. Remember, we're having a major rehearsal this afternoon. You're looking a little down after the audition."

"I don't know. Maybe we shouldn't be skipping class for the rehearsals anymore."

"And then what?" He pulled out a filtered cigarette from his pocket and lit it. "Grab one for yourself." He threw me the whole pack.

"Sit in class and try to learn something. The whole country is talking about college. My cousin in Shanghai is attending a crash course to prepare for the entrance exams."

"And *you're* thinking of college?" He looked at me, surprised.

"What do you mean by that?"

"I mean, when was the last time you did your homework?"

"There's always time."

"No time can make up for that. We're two years behind everything. And this is a lousy school to begin with. The teachers are suckers. Good thing I don't have to depend on them."

"Right, you can always go and become a driver."

"I'll make you a driver too. I really could try my dad on that one," he said, smiling. "Here, smoke."

I pushed his hand away.

The bell rang. The first class was English.

"Let's go in, I-Fei."

"You go ahead; let me finish smoking," he said coolly, a little grumpy at my new attitude.

I threw myself inside through our usual route, the window, and landed right in my seat. The teacher was leaning against the desk, trying to catch his breath. His glasses slipped to the tip of his nose and his beady eyes were looking around but not seeing anything. Boys and girls were still talking noisily. The teacher commanded no respect. He didn't care. He weighed two pieces of chalk in his hands.

One he held like a cigarette, the other was to throw at the most badly behaved student in class. You could count on being hit right on the tip of your nose.

"To what do I owe this honor, Mr. Da?" the teacher asked.

I ducked down. I hadn't been to his class for a long time.

"No rehearsal today?" The teacher threw the chalk at me. It landed on my head.

The class laughed.

I stayed down, quiet.

"If you had let me know earlier, I could have prepared something special for you, like an ABC lesson." He laughed along with the class and, as usual, ended up coughing until his face turned blue. He leaned on the desk until the spasm passed.

I felt embarrassed and ashamed, but I was angry, too.

Cough some more, you fool, I thought.

Outside the window, I-Fei was making a face at me, gesturing for me to join him.

"Yeah, why don't you just let yourself out and have a smoke with your pal down there?" The teacher caught his breath, then threw another piece of chalk at I-Fei, which hit his forehead.

Laughter again.

I could feel my face turn red, then white. I decided to leave the room and never return. As I crossed the threshold, I heard him say, "Now we can start our lesson."

I-Fei had already lit a cigarette for me. Quietly I took a long drag as soon as I was out of the teacher's sight.

"What did I tell you?" I-Fei said. "There's no place for us there. We might as well be the kind of students that we have always been."

"I wasn't always like this," I said, puffing.

"I know," I-Fei said. "You should have learned then what you know now."

"You know everything."

"You're my best friend. People told me things after we beat up that Han guy."

"I used to be a very good student."

"But you were a miserable wimp," he said.

"That wasn't my fault," I said harshly.

I-Fei changed the subject. "Suppose you *were* a good student. Do you think a college would take you?"

"Do you mean with my family background?" He nodded.

"But my aunt said it was regardless of one's family background."

"And you believe that?"

"Why shouldn't I?"

"Because my dad said it was just a pretense. There will be different standards for admission. This society isn't going to change that fast. No offense to you people." He shook his head and threw a stone at a passing bird as we left school for the day.

From then on, miserably, I carried my schoolbag, heavy with untouched books, heading for classes I didn't understand. I would ask this student and that student, humbly trying to catch up on my own. But the more I learned, the more I realized how much I had missed and the more depressed I got. I was too ashamed to talk about it to my parents or to any teachers, most of whom had given up on me by now.

But my parents had noticed that I had been spending more time in my room, using a kerosene lamp at night, looking at my textbooks, and occasionally gingerly trying out some English pronunciations. I often heard Sen and Mo Gong whistling outside my window to get my attention, but I tried to control myself.

One night, the whistling lasted longer and I knew they couldn't wait anymore.

"You've become a bookworm nowadays," Mo Gong said.

"You can't simply close the window and not answer us."

"What's going on, brother?" I asked.

"Well, Yi is leaving."

"Where's he going?"

"His grandpa is retiring from the factory and Yi is taking over his job as an office worker."

We walked to Yi's workshop, where there was a table of food waiting for us. Sen, Siang, and Yi rushed over, picked me up, and threw me onto the sawdust.

"The place is clean!" I exclaimed to Yi, dusting my coat. "You're really getting out of here?"

"Yeah. I was hoping you would get into the county performing troupe so that we could be working in Putien together."

"You have to go alone for now," I said.

"Let's celebrate our first breakthrough among the brothers," Sen said. "Yi, don't you ever forget us. I'm still the eldest."

"He's going to marry a fair-skinned Putien City girl and she's going to say she'll leave if you keep those dirty friends," Siang joked.

"Talk about marrying," Sen said, "Da, you should write a letter for Yi to his old master's daughter, Ping. Remember her? And tell her the news."

"Maybe in English," Mo Gong said. "I heard you making those funny sounds."

"Shut up, you," I said good-naturedly.

"Don't be shy. We want you to do good. I would want you, if anyone, to make us proud by being a college student," Sen said. "The rest of us are history. You're our only hope."

The party ended with us wrestling each other on the soft sawdust. I promised to go with Yi to his factory the next day and help him carry the luggage. We chatted about the future until midnight. I told them I wanted to go to college. They laughed and said if I could master the art of that four-stringed thing the name of which they still didn't quite know how to say, then I should have no problem. They were my true friends. There was a generous spirit among them, not jealousy. As I walked home alone in the darkness, whistling, I saw a star shine brilliantly over the top of our ancient pine tree to the east of Yellow Stone. I was like that, only a twinkle in the dark.

THIRTEEN

The western tip of Yellow Stone was all river and ancient lychee trees that dipped low in the water. In summer, straw-hatted boatmen poled along slowly between the green branches that were in their way. The lychees, ripe and juicy, burned red like the cheeks of a gaudily painted woman and made the branches droop even lower. Only cicadas disturbed the tranquillity.

In the crook of the river, where the houses thinned and the trees thickened, nestled a three-story white house with a red-tiled roof. A tall wall fenced it off. It was a small world within itself. The entrance stayed closed at all times. Only the tops of papaya trees could be seen from the outside. The little white house belonged to twin sisters, the Weis, who were Baptists and had never married. In the town where Buddha called the shots, the little white house by the river was a symbol of something alien yet sacred.

People said the twins read the Bible in the sun and prayed

under the moonlight. They lived a quiet life and paid for a maid to do the shopping and cleaning for them. Occasionally, they had visitors on weekends. Townspeople whispered that they were secretly involved in some sort of ceremony. Their father was one of the first Chinese Baptist ministers in Putien, and the twins had grown up in a Baptist church run by American missionaries. The Americans taught them English, and they went on to become English professors at a teachers' college in Fuzhou. When the college closed down, they retired into the country, where their father had held the first Sunday service in the history of Yellow Stone.

The white-haired twin sisters enjoyed a special status among the townspeople. They were the closest thing to real Westerners. Those few who had been inside the home had had a glimpse of a mysterious life behind those closed doors.

The old vegetable man claimed to have heard the twin sisters talking in "the language of the red hair," probably English, one day when he was making a delivery. It was gentle, like singing, he said. The old cleaning lady insisted that the twins only used forks and knives. It puzzled the local people. It was such a terribly unlucky thing to do, using a knife at the dining table. Maybe it was the different god they believed in who helped them ward off the consequences of all the wrong things they did.

One day, after dark, we heard a gentle knocking at our door.

Dad opened it. Outside stood the white-haired Professor Wei, one of the twin sisters. Upon recognizing her, Dad took a step back.

"May I come in, please?" Her voice was so gentle and sincere.

"Of course, of course." Dad opened the door wide and let her in.

She bowed and smiled sweetly at us. We put down our chopsticks and bowed back to her. She was a petite lady in her late sixties. Upright and dignified, she seemed taller than her mere five feet. Her white hair was braided and twisted into a bun in back, neat and elegant.

"How may I help you, Professor?" Dad asked politely. He gestured for us kids to leave the room. We hurried out, then stuck our ears against the closed door.

"Please forgive me for intruding at such a late hour." She took out a handkerchief and continued. "My poor dear sister has had a minor stroke, and now her mouth is twisted to one side. I have heard of your reputation. Can you please help her?"

"I am flattered." Dad rubbed his hands like a joyful kid. "I'll be more than happy to see what I can do." Dad was in his best mood when he was called upon to help others.

"Mother," he called out to my mom, as if he knew that we were behind the closed door listening to every single word, "get me the blue jacket and a flashlight. I need to go out." Mom hurried in with his jacket, the one with all his acupuncture needles. I passed him the flashlight he kept under his pillow.

"God bless you. You are a kind man, as they said. I don't know how to thank you, Dr. Chen."

"Please don't call me Doctor, just Ar Gang." Dad was beaming. He didn't know what to do with the "God bless you" part.

"We can wait until tomorrow morning. I just needed to let my poor sister know. If you agree to treat her, then she will sleep peacefully tonight."

"She needs to be seen as soon as possible," Dad said.

"Oh, how can I thank you all!" She turned and bowed to each of us again.

We all bowed back.

After Dad left, I told the others that he had made a mistake.

"What mistake?" Mom asked.

"Well, when Professor Wei said 'God bless you,' Dad should have said something polite back. I'm sure she was expecting it."

"And what should he have said?" Mom asked.

"Buddha bless you!" They all laughed.

We were all proud of Dad. This case would put him at another level.

I was sure he had chills crawling up his spine at being called a doctor by her. This was a landmark, a milestone in Dad's career. It would be whispered about for a long time to come.

The other twin had had a light stroke. Dad soon began to see some progress. He reported that she was able to utter her first clear sound after two weeks of intensive and painful treatment. She was resilient and cooperative.

To thank Dad, the twins insisted on paying him for his work, but Dad wouldn't hear of it. They asked him whether there was anything they could do for us in return. Dad said that the twins begged him to think of a way, otherwise they would feel bad.

One night I said to Dad, "Maybe they could teach me English in their spare time."

He looked up from his medical book and stared thoughtfully at me for a second. "That's a wonderful idea. But your level might be a little too low for them. They taught in college, remember?"

"Maybe they won't mind," I begged.

"I could try. Son, how did you come up with such an idea?"

"Well, they have been trying to find a way to thank you."

"Yeah, but tell me why you thought of it." He put aside his book.

"They talk about college in school. I have no future. I'm not doing well, and I'm a couple of years behind. Other subjects are easier to make up, and I'm working on it, but no one can help me with English."

"What about the English teachers?"

"They made fun of me when I went back to their classes. Besides, their pronunciation is terrible. Each time my teacher reads English, he sounds like he's choking on a fishbone. He spits and gets red-faced. I don't think Englishmen talk like that."

Dad laughed. "Now, son, if you do get to study with Professor Wei, I want you to make at least as much effort as you did with the flute," he said seriously.

I nodded.

That night, before falling asleep, I blew out the light, knelt down on the pillow, and kowtowed to Buddha to beg for help. For the first time, I didn't know what to ask for. I buried my face in the soft pillow until I began to stifle myself. I murmured in my head the word *college,* but I could feel my face blush with shame for even thinking about it. College was for the superior few who not only had extreme intelligence but diligence, too. What was I? That night I dreamed about being sent to a remote farm where I was forced to dig a rocky hill until I collapsed. I woke up in the middle of the night in a cold sweat.

FOURTEEN

As the summer vacation drew near, Dad came back one day with the good news that Professor Wei would be willing to help tutor me in English. However, she would be away in Fuzhou for a couple of months, accompanying her sister, who would be in rehabilitation under the care of some famous doctors. She would see me when she returned.

I was happy and nervous at the same time. It gave me the whole summer to prepare, so maybe I wouldn't look too stupid. I drew up a study plan, leaving very little time for music or anything else.

A few days later, I-Fei rode his bike to my home and stopped briefly to tell me that he was leaving Yellow Stone for good and was transferring to another high school. Or maybe he would become a driver soon. He was extremely mysterious and his eyes kept looking beyond me. I asked him to stay for a while and chat about the old days, but he said it was a long way to travel to his mom's. So off he went, without regret. I was deeply hurt. He had been a loyal friend and great to be with. School would not be the same without him.

One day, when the remote Ching Mountain was wrapped in layers of lingering clouds that looked like a woman's hair flying loose in the wind, the commune sent an announcement over the loudspeaker system to warn the farmers of an impending typhoon. Suddenly all was chaos. The brigade leader banged on every member's door, urging the villagers to head for the fields and harvest the rice. All of it, even that which was still green, was to be cut rather than be ruined in the flood.

My eldest sister was away in Han Jian, working at her temporary job in the canned food factory—a violation of the commune's no-working-out-of-town-in-harvesttime rule. Dad asked me if I could step in and do her work, so the next day, while it was still dark, Mom awakened me at dawn. My brother, Jin, and my two sisters, Huang and Ke, were already at the dining table stuffing themselves with fried rice by the bowlful and washing it down with the soup Mom had been preparing since midnight. My brother, now a veteran farmer at the age of twenty-two, could eat as many as three large bowlfuls before going to work. Everyone worked fourteen-hour days, and Jin couldn't stand being hungry in the fields. After burping a few times, he lit a cigarette and put on his straw hat, ready to go.

I had stuffed as much food into my mouth at four in the morning as I could. Mom had warned me that I wouldn't eat again until one in the afternoon. With my eyes half-closed, I smelled the freshly simmered rice as though it were still a sweet dream.

"Follow me, little brother." After I, too, had burped with

satisfaction, Jin gave me a sickle and out I went, barefoot, into the dark fields.

The edge of the sky was whitish, as if someone had barely lifted the lid off the earth. We walked in silence among the weeds and grasses still wet with dew. I dragged my feet, fighting the fatigue of being woken at such an ungodly hour, a time when I should have been having the sweetest dreams. I stumbled blindly after my brother, the leader of the group, who whistled, hummed, and smoked as casually as if it were just another day.

"Here we are. We have about five *mus* [about one acre] of rice to cut before the sun sets." He pointed at the endless stretch of rice fields looming in the whitish dark. "The four of us will go in rows. I'll take the widest, then Ke and Huang will take the rows beside me. You, little brother, go slow and rest when you need to. Try to see if you can do that slice." He indicated the edge of a huge plot and smiled at me.

"No problem. Give me more," I said.

Jin showed me how to cut the tall rice stalks at their base and stack them behind me. He warned me not to cut my fingers in the dark. I stepped into the muddy, wet field, making a squishing noise. Some frogs and wild rats ran at the sound. Mosquitoes and insects hummed constantly around my nose, eyes, and ears, and I had to keep batting them away. I could feel the little worms and eels slithering away from under my toes. I closed my eyes and tried to think of something pleasant. The violin.

I grabbed big handfuls of stalks and cut them fiercely. My sisters stopped to check on me once in a while and were pleased with what I was doing. Soon the sun rose above the horizon and the endless fields gave off steam as the morning light embraced them. The rest of the land was still asleep.

The knee-high rice plants with needle-sharp leaves got in the way of my face and neck as I bent down. The fuzzy blades needed only to brush my skin to leave behind a red kiss. Soon the summer sun turned from gentle to glaring. Sweat beaded my forehead and trickled down into my eyebrows. My skin began to itch as though it were being attacked by thousands of slimy, crawling creatures angry that I had invaded their world with my sickle. I unbuttoned my drenched shirt and peeled it off, wiping my cut, sweaty face with it before tossing it behind me. I clenched my jaw to keep from yelling out loud at the pain of my burning skin. I didn't want my sisters and brother to think that their little brother wasn't farmer material. As I stretched my sore back, feeling like the old hunched merchant next door who didn't know what the sky looked like anymore, I saw that they were already thirty yards ahead of me, tirelessly bending over the rice that only seemed to end where the sky launched a rainbow.

My sisters and brother had grown up farming. I had seen them carry on their shoulders more than a hundred pounds of animal manure, to be used for fertilizer in the fields. Their skinny legs had trembled beneath the weight, but they dared not slow down for fear of criticism by the commune leaders, who were especially harsh to them. They had all endured, their teeth gritted. Brother Jin had once had a rusty nail go through his right foot. It took two months to heal. Huang had once become so dehydrated under the baking sun that she had passed out. And they all complained of constant back pain, but they had to push themselves on, for the commune would not allow any leaves of absence. Their food ration would have been withheld until those absences were made up. They had all grown tall, thin, and tanned like coconuts.

As I stood there watching them, I felt respect and fear. A

future as a farmer stretched out before me like the brutal fields. There would be endless toiling under a cruel sun, all for a meager existence that consisted of rice porridge and pickled vegetables. There would be hunger for at least three months a year, during which even the moldy yams became treasures on the dining table.

"Have a rest, brother," I heard Jin shout at me. His voice sounded tiny in that enormous field. "You don't have to hurry."

"Put your shirt back on or the sun will kill you," Ke said, standing up to take a look at me.

"I'm fine, you guys." But my mind was saying, *Let me go home.* I was sick of it already. I dropped my sickle and drummed my back with my fists, imitating my dad when he had had a hard day. I sighed at the narrow stretch of rice still before me, standing proud and nodding lazily in the occasional breeze. Slowly I bent my cracking back to pick up the sickle again, this time resting my elbows on my knees like a pregnant woman and hacking the plants stem by stem. I wished the sun would go down faster so that we could all go home and rest, but it stayed eternally motionless, a taunting fireball in the cloudless sky. Then I wished the rice would all fall on its back by itself.

The sun hung high above my head, and my back felt hot. Even the wet mud in the field was lukewarm, and the proud rice stems began to droop beneath the blaze, tired and sleepy. The day was only half done, but I was totally exhausted. My back hurt, my legs trembled, my face was covered with cuts, and my hands were a mass of raw blisters. I was so miserable I even didn't feel the walls of my stomach rub against each other. There was a burning in my throat that would take a whole fire brigade to snuff out. I felt angry, belittled, and pathetic. I could not beg to get out of my duty. It was just not done in the Chen family. We all worked hard together and played together. Mom and Dad would never approve of my giving up in the middle of my task. I hung on a few more yards; then the blisters burst. The raw flesh looked red and stung like needles. I heard my sister call my name.

"Little brother, come eat." I saw my mom stumbling along the edge of the field, carrying our lunch on a long bamboo pole. Her face was red beneath her straw hat.

I was so grateful to see her.

"Come wash your hands and eat, young farmer." Mom smiled at me as I dragged my feet toward her. The beautiful smile on her face was the highest praise she could give us. My sisters and brother gathered around Mom, who was pouring water from a bucket and passing out wet towels.

"You're not doing too bad at all. With your help, we will finish before dark." My brother beamed, slapping my back.

I screamed before I could stop myself.

"What's the matter? Did you burn your back?" Huang asked.

I was silent.

"I told you to leave your shirt on," she said.

"It was wet." They looked at me.

"Let me see your hands," Jin said. I held them out. The blisters continued to ooze. "Pack up and go home after lunch, okay? I'm sorry, it must hurt like hell." Mom and my sisters were upset. My mother hurriedly cleaned my bloody hands with a wet towel.

"I'm sorry, guys. But I can finish my share."

"No, go home and take care of your hands."

I was ashamed, feeling like a defector.

"It happened to me, too, when I started out." Jin extended

his hands. "Now look at them. They feel like iron. Go home and try to be a good student. Maybe someday you'll go to college and won't have to do hard work like this anymore. You can still shoot for it. The rest of us are too old for that." He looked at my sisters.

On our way home, I trailed behind Mom in silence, holding both my hands gingerly stretched out.

"Do you still want to be a farmer?" Mom asked.

I shook my head.

"Then study hard. You can choose your future; your sisters and brother can't. You're lucky. If they had blisters like yours, they would still have to be there till the last stem was harvested. It's their life."

Mom's words stayed with me for a long time.

The smell of soil and a vague other scent permeated the endless, brutal fields. I wouldn't miss it if I were never to return. The beauty of nature and the muddy fragrance at harvest used to fill me with emotion. Now the fields looked like a graveyard, filled with hungry ghosts that grabbed at my arms and legs. I didn't want to have my youth and future buried here.

As I followed Mom home, I felt a strong desire to start lessons with Professor Wei, to go back to school. There was a future somewhere for me other than hoes and sickles. There should be no hardship at school that I couldn't overcome. I was never more determined than at that moment. I felt fortunate. As Mom and Jin had said, I still had a chance.

The pain in my back and hands throbbed, but all I felt was gratitude for my family and a desire to succeed at school.

FIFTEEN

In late August, the lotus leaves floated lazily on the calm surface of the Dong Jing River. The clouds seemed distant, and in the fields, drab after the harvest, buffalo ducked their horns and pulled the heavy plows, bearing the weight on their callused shoulders, tossing up the flattened soil in readiness for the new plantings. They mooed—a sound the farmers interpreted as a prediction of rain for the following day.

Their brethren, a few acres away, joined in, and soon the whole buffalo community was mooing, like foxes howling in the high western mountains on a night lit by a full moon. Autumn filled me with emptiness, as if my heart knew the bleak winter was near. The sound of the buffalo always seemed to me the lonesome song of Yellow Stone's autumn. I used to sit by the river and stare at the buffalo in the distance, letting their song take me back to the distant memory of the summer now behind me, leaving me forlorn and melancholy.

One morning, Mom woke me and told me to put on a clean shirt because Professor Wei would like to start her lessons with me. I jumped out of bed like a young fish frolicking in shallow waters under the sun. I washed my face with soap, brushed my teeth three times, with a double load of toothpaste, and combed my hair into neat furrows, parted on the right. I even looked into details such as nose hair and earwax for five minutes in front of the broken half-mirror in my room.

I carried my English book in my schoolbag and walked along the deserted alley instead of the broad street for fear of getting teased by my friends, who usually took up their positions at the bridge and laughed at every soul who passed. If they had seen me, they would have roughed up my hair and tried to make me smoke until I smelled like a smokestack.

As I neared the western end of town, I became more self-conscious. My voice would sound too loud or too provincial. Even my toes seemed funny, sticking out of the sandals. The breeze had blown my way and no doubt my hair looked like a bird's nest by now. I touched it lightly with my fingers. It felt all wrong. I squatted by the river and checked my wavering image in the water. A few strands of hair were sticking up. I pasted them down with water and opened my mouth wide to make sure no food was stuck in my teeth. Then I ran along until I stood in front of the forbidding door to the Weis' estate. Only after I had caught my breath did I knock, cautiously.

I heard the low rumble of a dog. It was sniffing away behind the door, becoming excited as it caught my scent. It seemed to say, *"Welcome to the Wei estate, and could I have your ass for lunch?"* I took a step backward and almost peed in my pants.

"Shhh . . . be polite." A gentle female voice came from behind the door. The dog growled some more and barked grumpily. I took another step back. Politeness was not quite the issue here; he wanted to eat me.

"You are a naughty dog today, go sit in your house." The voice became firmer this time. Gee, how about locking him up? He was only a flesh-eating animal. He dragged his feet away, shuffling along the ground, reluctantly leaving. No doubt his eyes still lingered on the door, no doubt he was still full of evil thoughts about having me for lunch. After all, it was a man-eat-dog or dog-eat-man world out there.

The door opened and a white-haired Professor Wei smiled like a white lily in full bloom.

"Come in, please," she said in English.

My mind rapidly searched for an answer. I knew "Sit down, please." Our teacher used to say that sarcastically whenever I stood scratching my head, unable to answer any of his questions. Professor Wei wanted me to do something, but I did not know what. I didn't know whether to step forward or backward, to nod or to shake my head, until she gestured with her hand for me to come in.

"Thank you, thank you." I used up the only other two English words I knew in one single sentence, then cut my eyes left and right, looking for the fabled animal, who was probably whetting his teeth on stone and ratcheting his appetite up for my skinny behind.

"It should not be 'Tank you.' It should be 'Thank you,' with the tip of your tongue between your teeth," she said as I followed her into the garden.

It was the first time I had opened my big mouth and I had already tanked her instead of thanking her. This was going to be great. She might as well return me to the other side of the wall, where I belonged.

But she smiled, showing a shallow dimple in her lined face, like a sweet little girl trapped inside wrinkled makeup. "I like your hair. Nowadays, kids just don't comb their hair like they used to." I blushed. I understood her this time; she had switched to Chinese.

Had it not been for the river outside, my hair would have been sticking out like a sprouting onion garden. I was thankful. First impressions were important. I wondered what she would have said had my hair been less than perfect. Then there would surely have been nothing positive left about me in her eyes. She was doing this because she felt she and her sister owed my dad. That was it. I wouldn't be surprised if she told me after the first lesson that I was as impossible to educate as that dog out there. He probably understood more English than I did after all the eavesdropping he did from his own little house.

"Come on in, don't worry about the floor, and sit down here." She pointed to a cozy couch.

Good thing she spoke in Chinese or I would have mistaken it as an order to take off my sandals and crawl on my knees to avoid touching her floors with my dirty feet. I tiptoed across the living room, making my footprints as faint as possible. As I sank into the sofa, I was surprised how deep down I went. It wrapped my bottom snugly like no other chair I had ever sat in. I felt cradled by the touch of something soft and velvety. A sense of undeserved comfort swept over me.

Professor Wei pulled a chair over next to me. I straightened up from my own like a puppet pulled by its strings. She put her hand on mine to keep me from jumping out of my seat.

"I was very glad to hear from your lovely dad that you wanted to study English with me. What a refreshing idea!" She tossed her silver head and her eyes filled with a soft glow. Then her voice changed ever so slightly. "Nowadays, kids out there only do bad things like smoking, gambling, fighting, and worse, talking about girls at such young ages." I shifted uncomfortably in my seat and felt the pack of Flying Horse in my back pocket; I was going to light a cigarette just as soon as I was out of there. The urge to smoke was alive and kicking.

"Now, why don't you show me how much English you know and I'll design a program for you." She crossed her legs and placed her hands one on top of the other on her knees, comfortable in her role as audience.

I knew the time of embarrassment had come. I fumbled in my schoolbag and fished out the untouched English book. I regretted not tearing out the second page, all scribbled over with caricatures of my English teacher.

"Read me the alphabet." That wasn't a bad place to start.

I cranked along with my rusty pronunciation, more and more unsure the further I went. I was red-faced at *G*, sweating at *H*, trembling at *I,* and lightheaded at *J.* The English sounds seemed to block my air passage, and my lips went dry. I almost choked on those strange, vocal-cord-twisting letters. She stopped me just in time.

"It's hard, isn't it?" I nodded, red-faced and mortified.

"I don't want you to pronounce those letters from your imagination. You made up some of the sounds as you went along, didn't you? Now, follow me." She half closed her eyes and read each letter slowly.

"A, B, C, D, E." She stopped and looked at me. "You made *E* sound like *A*. Now try again." Her voice was like music to my ears. I wondered how different my life would have been had my goldfish-eyed teacher in school had one tenth of her elegance.

I imitated the movements of her mouth. She stopped at *E,* tilted her head, and listened quietly as I went over the letter until I beat it to death. Then she nodded reluctantly. We moved on.

The last letter, *Z,* took us a good three minutes. No matter how hard I stretched my neck, I could not get it. She looked at me patiently, with a slight frown, like a doctor trying to decide which remedy to use. I felt totally useless and stupid.

"So much for today." She was declaring me a failure. I wasn't wanted back—because of my dirty feet and ignorance, I was sure. She was going to give a weak excuse to spare me, but when I was gone, she would say to herself in English, *What a terrible kid! Not only ignorant, but also impossible to cultivate. Perfect farmer material.* My head went wild.

"You are very, very smart, I can tell from our first lesson." She cupped her tiny hands, which were still beautiful, under her elegant chin. "I am full of hope for you," she said. "If only you would come every day." Her eyes were glowing with light as she looked at me. She was asking me to come back; I couldn't believe it. Hope filled me up again as if I were a sagging balloon. I was ready to fly.

I collected my bag and backpedaled toward the door, where my dear old friend the dog was staring at me. He breathed angrily through his dark wet snout. *You were lucky to stay that long and still be breathing,* he seemed to say. He looked disdainful now. He had heard my terrible pronunciation, so bad that it had ruined his appetite. He, the defender of the elegant, wanted to kill me for mangling such a beautiful language.

You loser, don't ever come back again. His ears popped up, his eyes narrowed.

"Be a good boy, back to your house," Professor Wei said gently. The monster dragged his bushy tail and shot a hateful look at me over his shoulder before heading for his house. What a character—did I have to deal with this grump every single day? When would it end? The day I lost my ass to him? I picked my way gingerly behind the monster, darted through the door, and let out a huge sigh as I fished out a Flying Horse. My eyes darted around, making sure Professor Wei wasn't witnessing another deadly sin from her lofty window upstairs. I would have waited if I could, but my vocal cords were screaming with desire to be smoked red and blue, and my heart throbbed with the excitement of surviving this landmark day. I needed to calm down or I would find myself jumping into the cool river. I was overcome with mixed feelings of joy and sadness. This was a new start to my boring and hopeless life, but it would be a long, uphill ride from the very bottom. The hill was Everest and I was starting out somewhere under the Pacific Ocean.

SIXTEEN

造

The school was without I-Fei now, and I had stopped going to the rehearsals. My classmates stared at me as though I were a dinosaur. Most of them hated me because I was arrogant, pompous, and too much of an artistic star. In elementary school, they would have gotten together and beat me up, but times had changed. I was the big guy, sitting in the backseat, angry, ignorant, a fallen star of yesterday, a hostile sight to avoid. They cold-shouldered me. The rest of the school carried on as if I weren't there. I watched them disdainfully and quietly. A few smaller guys in class still speculated that I had dated the most beautiful girl in the school's performing troupe. They winked at me when they saw her pass our classroom window. I said nothing and kept them guessing in order to maintain the last ounce of respect I commanded among the students.

Dia was one of the guys who warmed up to me after he saw the vacancy left behind by I-Fei. He was a thin fellow who seemed to jump rather than walk. He had monkey ears and his hair was always a messy lawn that seemed as if it hadn't been mown for ages. He lived in a poor village ten miles west of Yellow Stone and walked to school every morning at sunrise, returning home at about eight each night. He was one of those kids known around the school as walkers to distinguish them from the students who bunked at the school dorm. He was the only person I knew who made thicker and longer tobacco rolls than Yi. And he used old newspaper to roll them. Sometimes when he ran out of old newspaper he would run around school looking for any scrap paper he could find.

This thin little guy carried a large schoolbag with him during the course of the day. Most of the space in it was taken up by the two cold meals he had to carry around, and the rest was divided up equally between books, a bag of foul-smelling homegrown tobacco, and an ugly pipe made from a twig. His nicotine addiction was legendary. He was the only person I knew who smoked before and after each meal and stopped halfway to squeeze in another thick, long to-bacco roll.

The more time I spent with Dia, the less I felt like smoking at all. He was a great example of what happens to smokers. At the age of fifteen, he had a chronic cough and spit up sticky green stuff like an old man of ninety. His lungs wheezed loudly through his bony chest, outlined by countable ribs. His teeth were dark in front and back and he had a pale, lifeless look. The only gleam in his eye came from the reflected light of the matches with which he lit his rolls.

"How can you smoke like that?" I asked once, after we became better friends.

"Look who's talking." Dia stared at me, puzzled. "What's wrong with me?"

"Well, the tobacco and the old newspapers you're using will kill you soon."

"I'm not dying anytime soon, Da. Grandpa rolled his first roll at the age of four and he's still kicking. He taught Dad to smoke at the age of five and *he's* still breathing. I didn't smoke till seven. The Dias are living legends. We'll live on."

Every morning he made his first stop at my house, after his ten-mile walk. I treated him to some hot tea. He would sneak to our backyard for a smoke and then reappear refreshed. Then we walked to school together. In the afternoon, he played with me for a while before the long journey home. Some weekends I would offer him my bunk bed so that he could stay for a night. He fought the invitations valiantly, but in the end never refused the offers. When he slept over, we talked about our lives and future late into the night. He wasn't a demanding guest; all he required was a chair to step on so that he could climb to the attic windowsill like a cat and smoke in the open air while staring at the bright stars.

The midterm exams came sooner than I liked. It was the first time I was paying attention to them. It had been a breezy school without serious tests for years. Now that concept was arcane. The good students in class applauded and chatted excitedly about how they were going to review courses and score well. The losers put their heads on the desks and drummed the desktops, hating every word uttered by the good students.

The teacher enthusiastically answered questions the good

students raised, and even threw in a smile or two when it came to the pretty girls in class. But when I raised my hand and asked which English book we would be tested on, the whole class burst into uncontrollable laughter.

It was a big joke. The good students huddled together and laughed. Enjoying my humiliation, the teacher leaned back in his chair.

"What do you think?" he said slowly, tossing the chalk in his hands.

More laughter.

"I don't know."

"Since when did you become interested in tests? Shouldn't you be in rehearsal at this time of the day?" He looked at his watch, smirking. "For your information, it will be book four that you will be tested on. Are you sure you have book four in your possession?" Continued laughter.

I felt Dia's eyes on me. He was the only one feeling sorry for me.

The rest of them probably thought I was a drunk, just waking up to the glaring sunlight. I was human garbage in their eyes, victimized by changing times, with no idea of how to pull myself out of the hole I had sunk into. The talents I had, playing the flute and violin, were talents of yesterday. Now it was college, and whoever could jump through the hoop and be that lucky one percent to go on to college was the hero of the day. I still stank with yesterday's staleness. Most of them were happy to see me fall on my face, hoping I would break a few bones in the process.

The tests offered scant surprises. I stared at each paper for a good five minutes, scribbled down something, and turned them in. I answered half the questions on the math test with ease, but the rest looked like a foreign language. And I only did one third of the physics test. History and geography were the hardest subjects to guess on, and whatever English I had mastered from the professor, a secret, was a mere scratch on a pyramid. Chinese was the only subject I excelled in. I had studied classics with my grandpa.

At the end of the week of tests, I felt as if I had gone to the Olympics and ended up sweeping the floor after everyone had left. I was sad, angry, and lost. What was I going to do with my life?

SEVENTEEN

造

Dia and I found a new spot behind the school wall, where we met and chatted as he polluted his lungs with dark tobacco. He told me the secret of the Dia tobacco. Since his grandpa's time, they had kept a plot of land in their backyard the size of a basketball court, where they grew broad-leaved tobacco. The rich, bitter flavor was attributed to the fact that young Dia each morning watered the plants with the contents of three full night pots used overnight by the men in the Dia household. The thick, smelly piss nourished the young plants and added a special flavor not found with other growers. Thus Dia's brand worked like a double-barreled shotgun, powerful and potent. It remained the only tobacco known to be able to quench their nicotine addiction, not a small feat.

"Have a smoke." Dia sat down and rolled me a thick one.

"No thanks, not after you told me the piss story."

"You'll need some sorta smoke for what I gotta tell you." It sounded bad. I looked into his eyes and he looked down. I took the roll and let him light it for me. Instantly, I felt the potent kick. The Dia piss worked miracles. I spat like a fisherman. "What's the matter?"

"The midterm grades are out." He had a dead man's tone, flat.

"How are ours?" I could feel my heart begging for mercy from the good Buddha. *Make it presentable,* I promised him, *and I'll give you another thousand kowtows this very night.*

"Well, mine are terrible."

"And?"

"Yours are real bad." Kowtowing wouldn't be necessary anymore. I had hit bottom and I deserved it. I puffed on the bitter smoke. For the first time, I felt good as I inhaled. I felt the rush go to my head; it was comforting, and I was satisfyingly numb. I leaned back on the red dirt wall limply, like a piece of smashed tofu. There wasn't an ounce of strength left in my body.

I was a failure, shaming myself and my family. I should change my last name and never return home to beg for meals anymore. Maybe I would take to the road like Mo Gong and Siang. The burden of failure made me despise myself.

"That's not all," Dia added, stealing a careful look at me.

"What do you mean?"

"Someone pasted the results of all your exams on the wall outside our classroom. Now the whole school knows."

"Son of a whore! It must be our principal teacher." I gritted my teeth and slammed my fists into the soil. Now I was the laughingstock of the whole school. All my enemies, old and new, would be rejoicing over my downfall. Not only was I the son of a landlord, but I was stupid and lazy. Wise people could forgive the former but not the latter. I had shamed my whole family tree.

My family of tired young farmers would have no patience when the only student in the household came home with disgraceful academic results. They worked their butts off in the fields, callused their hands, bent their young backs, and lost their dream of being young. I had been wasting my time smoking, playing around, and not making use of the great opportunity offered me. It was a sin they couldn't have afforded to commit.

With my head bent and eyes downcast, I stumbled into our dining room. The whole family stopped talking as I entered.

Silence.

I deserved it. I slid into my seat and stared at the tip of my chopsticks, eating carefully so that they didn't clink on the edge of the bowl and anger anyone. I heard myself slurp in the rice. The silence was getting heavier with each passing second.

Dad scooped a big spoonful of green beans into my bowl. It was a good sign. The head of the family had spoken with his action. I stole a look at him. He looked back.

"You broke a record, they say." I was quiet.

"It's time you do something about it. Your brother here wants to take time off to prepare for the college exam, but the commune won't allow him. Even if they do allow him, we're not sure we could do without his food rations." He pointed at the rice that was getting cold in my bowl. I stared at it and my guts twisted with guilt and sorrow. I wished I were dead. If I had been the older one, I would have been out there hustling. I witnessed the hardships my brother and sisters endured every day. They were in their late teens and early twenties. They had no new clothes and no money, just bodies filled with aches and pains such as only older folks should have. But the worst was that they thought they would be forced to be farmers for life, unable to marry anyone else but another farmer, to bear another generation of lowly farmers, on into infinity.

The sun would never rise in their minds. It was modern-day slavery on the farm, with the promise of little in return. In contrast, all I did was go to school. And what had I achieved? A shameful performance.

"You have a year and a half to get your act together; the farming tools will all be ready and waiting for you in the pigsty, just in case." It sounded like probation. No improvement, and I would be condemned to a life sentence on the Communist farm. I looked up at everybody after the sentencing, feeling a load being lifted off my back.

They all wore mixed expressions of reproach and criticism, along with a touch of encouragement and even hope; the whole spectrum. I loved my family.

That night before going to sleep, I asked Mom to wake me at five from the following day on and every day afterward. I promised her that I would use the precious morning hours before breakfast, when my mind was uncluttered, to take a bite out of those unopened books of mine. She nodded thoughtfully, half doubting my sincerity.

I went to my room and knelt before the makeshift shrine to Buddha for a good ten minutes, not knowing what to beg from his benevolence. I was a total mess. Guilt ate away at my soul for goofing off what precious time I had before the national entrance examinations. I banged my head on the floor, swearing to work hard from then on. In the end, I became dizzy and went to sleep with a big smile on my face.

I was sure that Buddha, my smiling, chubby spiritual light, had heard me this time. I'd banged hard enough.

I figured that with eighteen months left until the national exam, I simply had to use every waking moment of my life for studying. It would be four years' worth of work squeezed into eighteen months. My life was over for the time being.

No friends, no movies, no chatting. No sitting in class passively awaiting the inept teacher to feed you. It had to be a flat-out attack on all the books I hadn't touched. I was going to breathe and live those books.

But which book should I start with? I looked at them, puzzled. I needed a scheme, a method, or I would never beat the competition. Only one out of a hundred made it in. I could easily kiss the books and my life good-bye and say hello to rice paddies.

A big official poster about the new college system was posted conspicuously on the wall of the commune's headquarters. Hundreds of young people traveled miles just to stand before it for hours, half believing what it said in black and white. Some copied it down on a small piece of paper and brought it back for others to see, as if they couldn't trust their memory. Confusion reigned among the people of Yellow Stone.

Only months ago, Chairman Mao had been alive and kicking on his sickbed under the loving care of his young nurses, who saw it as a heroic, patriotic act to mix their business with his pleasure. School was bad and revolution was good. Young people had gotten used to it. They liked it that way. They beat up the teachers, burned down schools, marched out of classes, and drank and smoked as they saw fit. There were no tests, no grades, no good students, no bad students. They were all bad, therefore all good. Everything was fine because Mao said so.

Now everything was upside down again. The announcement explained nothing. It didn't make any distinction between the children of the politically good and the politically bad families. It said the tests were open to all and that admission into college was based purely on performance.

Suddenly, everyone was talking about college. People gathered in knots, swapping gossip about who would be the most competitive in the tests. The bridge where my friends used to sit and chat about women and gambling was now a forum in which they discussed who the next math or English wizard might be. War stories about some legendary teachers from our high school began to circulate among the people of Yellow Stone.

There was the fat math teacher, Du, with bushy eyebrows and a birthmark as ugly and prominent as a dark cloud on a sunny day. Before the Cultural Revolution, each year on the day prior to the national college exam Mr. Du would call an emergency meeting for all the graduates, flip open a portable blackboard, and show the lengthy solutions to a few complicated math questions he predicted would appear as major score-gainers. He would come in and talk briefly but importantly for ten minutes. The meeting was over when he lit his cigarette.

Nervous students hurriedly jotted down all the details and committed them to memory. Du's track record had been consistent: eight out of ten. Marginal students had been brought to tears when they saw the questions appear on the real exam.

Then there was the history teacher, Mr. Wa, who was no pretty boy either. He looked frighteningly like someone from the Pleistocene age, minus the thick body hair. All he needed to do to give us a living picture of Peking man was to bend his back a little, walk slowly in front of the class, and let his long arms dangle on both sides. His head had only two parts, the forehead and the chin. His eyes gleamed wildly under a steep cliff of a forehead, and his small nose flattened out above a set of teeth so big that he had a hard time closing his mouth. He spoke in a stutter, spattering everything around him with saliva. His voice roared like Peking man's must have done, seemingly unaccustomed to the gentility of evolution.

And then there were the superstudents, who had attended high school before the Cultural Revolution and had a solid foundation in all the subjects. Among them were my cousin Tan and a neighbor by the name of Li. Candidates worked on old college exam questions; these guys breezed through effortlessly. In the eyes of youngsters like me, they were heroes.

As the first national examination drew near, the talk of legends stopped. Everyone watched silently as the candidates nervously awaited their date of trial.

On the first day of the examination, pale students walked toward the test sites, quiet and anxious. Mr. Du called for a meeting. So did the Peking Man. The meetings were open to all. Thousands of students crowded into the high school's open-air gym and listened through crackling loudspeakers to the two legends at work. The atmosphere was as sacred as at a religious event, and hearts were just as pious.

At 9:00 A.M., I put down my books and joined the rest of the crowd to watch the uniformed county police ride into town on three-wheeled motorcycles, carrying the examination papers. The street was quiet as the police honked their way noisily through the thick crowd.

Hours later, some of that crowd would be winners and many would be losers. I held my head between my hands and sneaked back to my room. I felt weak in the knees just thinking about those poor guys who opened up their papers and registered a blank. One of them could be me. It had definitely been me at midterm. I buried my head hopelessly among my books, then stared out the window.

EIGHTEEN

I was making slow progress. Math, physics, and chemistry were hard.

I was behind a couple of years, and the formulas seemed to have gotten longer since I'd last studied them. The teacher was lecturing on calculus and matrices, while I was still struggling to catch up on geometric equations. I attended the classes. The teacher and the good students treated me as if I didn't exist. Each time I raised my hand, there was an uncomfortable hush in the room. Another stupid question. My math teacher would roll his eyes and reluctantly give me the chance to ask my question. Then he would ask his protégé, the Head, to answer it.

"The Head" was a nickname we gave to the class president, who had a huge, shiny forehead. He was also the school's Communist Youth League president. He was the kind of guy who made exaggerated speeches in public meetings and shouted slogans while parading on National Day. He walked with a stiff neck and a pair of duck feet. He looked at other lowly classmates with disdain and was considered the biggest snob on campus. He was doing fine among other equally snobbish highfliers until the day he was caught writing a love letter to a girl in class. Now he was in another league, a womanizer and a snob.

When the Head was done, the teacher applauded slowly, nodding and smiling. Another superb performance by his young talent. The teacher himself was distantly cool. He openly avoided talking to me, such a lowly student. Once was enough, but again and again? I quickly lost interest in his class. My mind wandered off on dangerous paths.

Ideas flitted around inside my head about how best to torture such an evil being. It would have been fitting to have him and his protégé tied up, buck naked, to the old pine tree at the school entrance and let them beg for mercy as the chilly sea wind nipped at their skin. I hated them and I hated myself.

One day I went down to our storage room, which was decorated with spiderwebs and housed hundreds of unknown, lethal crawling creatures. Flashlight in hand, I kicked and fumbled among legless, armless pieces of furniture. It was my cave; there were treasures to be explored. I had Grandpa's old gambling lamp in mind. It was a huge, infamous object with ornate bronze designs and had been given to him by his gambling buddy to prevent cheating in the dark. It was put in storage because of its gigantic appetite—it burned a whole bottle of oil a night, and its smoke stained the white mosquito nets black.

I flashed the light around the dark room; in the corner my old friend glistened like a beacon at sea. As I stepped over cautiously, my big toe caught a round thing that rolled until it hit the wall with a healthy clang. I turned the light onto it, and there, standing on its bottom, was an aged, elegant pot shaped like a short, flat pumpkin. It was Grandpa's liquor jar. It used to sit on his lap and sleep by his pillow. He sipped blissfully from it when it was full and whistled into it when it was empty. It was his other child, the child Grandma didn't have any part of bearing. Nor was it one she approved of.

I scooped up both of Grandpa's legacies and dodged my way out, without ruining too many of the webs guarding the room.

"What are you doing with those things?" Mom asked. She had been standing by the door waiting for me.

"Well, I decided to study by myself in my room in the evenings, so I need a good lamp for light and a teapot." I clutched my two treasures.

Anything for my studies. Mom could have objected, but she didn't. She knew my ways of tackling a problem. If I danced around something long enough, I would eventually give it my total attention. Mom was a little goddess that the big god had sent into our lives. She understood my vices and tried to forgive me as much as her limited powers allowed her.

That night after dinner I officially locked my door, lit my big lamp, and filled up the old jar with dark, steaming tea. I made sure a night pot stood by, prepared to take a larger than usual output. I was ready to burn.

But as I picked up physics, I thought about chemistry. When I leafed through chemistry, the math book screamed for my attention. I fought the temptation of the green English book, which by now had become my favorite, and there were the books on history, geology, and philosophy moaning and groaning at the bottom of the pile like stepchildren.

Only Chinese history was a given. My midterm results in that subject put me legitimately at the top of the class. I juggled all these books like parts on an assembly line, finally dropping them and resting my head in the cradle of my hands.

Finally, I settled for the English book. I was showing decent progress, I was told. There were the usual vocabulary, grammar, drills, tests, and conversations. These simple conversations were silly but thought-provoking. I often wondered why Englishmen greeted each other with phrases like "Good morning," "Good afternoon," and "Good night." Simply "good" everything. If I walked around the dirt street of Yellow Stone and greeted people with the "good" formula, they would think I was crazy. Some might even knock my teeth out and ban me from the town forever. Those folks were content asking each other, "Have you had breakfast [or lunch or dinner] yet?" After all, nothing was "good" about a day till your stomach was filled.

I was awakened by Mom's knock on the door. It was five in the morning and I was in my bed, my English book still on my desk. The lamp had used up the whole bottle of oil. The teapot was empty. I had no recollection of undressing myself or putting the light out.

"How did I go to sleep last night?" I asked Mom, whose face was now inside my door.

"Dad saw your light still on at two and found you asleep with your face on the book." I must have drifted off. "No more irregular hours like that. You are going to ruin your health."

"But, Mom, I need to study longer hours to catch up."

"You won't catch up that way. You need to have a good, healthy schedule." Such intense conversation made my head throb. I slipped under the warm quilt and had another fifteen minutes in bed before I kicked off the blanket and splashed my face with icy water from the river.

One afternoon, as I was on my way to Professor Wei's house, the rain began to penetrate the thick foliage that covered the narrow road.

It was so loud and urgent, it sounded as if a machine gun were spraying the leaves with bullets. It saved me the trouble of bending down in the river to wet my hair. I combed my mop with my hands as I saw the thick clouds gathering on the western horizon. A storm was coming.

I skidded along the wet road and was happy to finally arrive at Professor Wei's door. It had been left open, and as I ran upstairs I could hear her voice coming from the second-floor window. She waved to me. I smiled back.

Not surprisingly, the dog was standing in the rain, greeting me with his mean dark glare. He dug his back feet firmly into the ground, as if warming up to attack me. He gave a throaty rumble, a weak threat that I had gotten used to, and blocked my way. There was something different in his eyes that day, a knowing look. I checked the second-floor window for help. Professor Wei was gone. It was just me and the dog, and he had the upper hand. I wished I had a rifle. The spot between his eyes looked very tempting.

He sniffed my thoughts and shook his head in defiance. Water splashed all over me. I shook my own head. Not as much water. The cunning animal was enjoying seeing me get drenched by the storm. He wanted to see me chilled, sneezing, then on the floor begging for mercy, at which time he would walk over and sink his teeth into a juicy part of me. A dinner in the rain was better than no dinner at all.

Sudden lightning cleaved the dark sky, followed immediately by deafening thunder no more than half a mile away. The loud sound brought me to my knees. I closed my eyes and plugged my ears with my thumbs, waiting for the imminent attack from both the thunder and the dog, but nothing happened. The thunder trailed down to spasmodic firecracker mutterings and vanished. I opened my eyes and saw the dog crawling in the mud toward his house, his tail tucked between his legs.

At that moment, I lost all respect for the animal and wanted to shoot myself for having put up with his cruel, unfair treatment.

Professor Wei greeted me with a dry towel as I sauntered toward the door like a real man for the first time, fearless and dignified. I could feel the weak look in the dog's eyes now that he had been brought to his knees by the thunder. I had withstood the uproar. I took the towel and gave my head a good drying. Professor Wei found me a T-shirt and I was once again comfortable. But no feeling surpassed the sweetness of winning. That dog was forever crossed off my fear list. It was, after all, a man's world out there, pal.

"You look happy today," Professor Wei said, rather surprised.

"Thank you, I'm happy to be here," I said in English.

"Maybe you know something already," she said in Chinese.

"What do you mean?"

"Well, I heard from my friend in Putien that for the next college examination, if you choose English as your major, you don't have to take tests in science or math at all."

"Is that right?" I pinched my thigh, almost jumping out of the seat.

I tried to imagine life without math, chemistry, and

physics. It would be like a honeymoon forever. I felt like standing up and singing an aria.

"Oh, but why?"

"Well, the government lacks English majors in all the major universities. I think you should shoot for a college in, say, Beijing." Beijing! Only the best went there. *Yes, ma'am, whatever you say!*

"You think I am going to be that good?"

"You will be if you work hard. You have shown tremendous progress."

"Really?"

"I am going to cram you until you are full."

Cram me, please. I never felt emptier.

"Here you go." She pulled out a bagful of books and printed papers. "These are the exercises and all the English vocabulary that you need to know to pass the test." She patted the stack like an insurance man talking about a rainy day.

I rushed over and touched the pile with a shaking hand. This would be my salvation.

The news about the college examinations worried my parents a great deal. It meant that I would give up my science courses. Was it premature? The government was changeable on policies like that. This was a country that had changed the constitution more often than its meals. There was intense conversation between my parents. I felt it necessary to drop in the key words.

"With this policy, I might be able to apply to study English in a college in Beijing." It was a showstopper. They were silenced. They looked at me with doubt.

But Dad thought about it for a second, then nodded with approval. "I like the sound of it." He was the man who had made me the first violin player in the history of Yellow

Stone, however bad I was, and he was ready for me to major in English and to send me off to Beijing. He would share every bit of my progress over tea with his many friends for the rest of his life.

Dad was the dreamer. Mom was the practical enforcer who knocked on the door at five every morning to wake me and shake the mosquito net, making sure I didn't take too long a nap between studies or waste time daydreaming.

"Wouldn't that be a little too fancy and exotic for us?" Mom asked.

You bet it would. Think mud, think manure, think digging the hills, that would be more appropriate for us, but I wanted to be special.

NINETEEN

Cousin Tan locked himself up in the attic on the day the results of the examinations came out. The pressure was so great that he hadn't eaten for days, and he had been suffering a mild depression since taking the test. He had tried alcohol. It didn't help. Then he had slept and slept, with the team leader laughing outside his window, calling him crazy. We were all worried. Then one day Tan had emerged suddenly, throwing himself into farmwork. He kept silent about the test and shut his mouth whenever anyone talked about college. He was an angry mute, immersed in his own world. He had lost weight and looked forty, even though he was only in his early thirties.

His excellent scores sent shock waves through Yellow Stone. Tan cried as the results were slipped under the door of his hideout. He at first refused to open the envelope. When he eventually did, he let out a piercing scream and danced downstairs to meet his beaming family.

He was the sort of guy born for college life. Nerdy, wearing thick glasses, he read everything, including the microscopic directions on the backs of chemical fertilizer bags. He wrote poetry and dabbled in fiction in his spare time. He was dreamy and romantic. Way beyond the marrying age, he had refused many matchmaking sessions with sorry-looking countryside girls. His vision of a wife existed only in books.

Considering he came from a landlord's family with no prospects whatsoever, he was lucky anyone would even consider him. The situation didn't trouble him a bit. He had made peace with himself. Why bother with marriage? Wait until you could afford it, he used to say, which frustrated the heck out of my uncle, who believed that by now he should have been surrounded by mischievous grandkids.

Two days after the results came out, Tan fell into another bout of depression. He said the high scores would only worsen his disappointment in the end. The scores were nothing but a cover-up. One's political background would take precedence. Such a drop from a staggering height would crush his soul. There were again rumors that candidates from the wrong families, despite high scores, would be placed at the end of the admission line. When all the slots were filled, they would be left holding an empty bag, just another way of finishing off the wrong families. Tan retreated into his attic and stared out the window all day long.

At the end of the summer, Tan became the first college student in Yellow Stone after the Cultural Revolution. Amoy University, finance major. When the certified admission letter arrived bearing his name, the whole town was stunned. Amoy University, located on the beautiful subtropical island of Amoy, was the best in Fujian. It trained the cadres for the province. It was an old boys' club. Tan would fit in beautifully.

This time, the whole family was teary-eyed. Many years of suffering had suddenly come to an end. The sun had risen and that night the stars would shine. Tan was now the happiest of men, giving Flying Horses away as if he were getting married. I eyed his slightly bent back and tired eyes. It wouldn't surprise me if some professors were younger than he. Maybe he, too, would become a professor and marry one of his female students. I was so happy for him.

From that point on, his fate changed dramatically. Tan received three wedding proposals in the next three days from the most eligible girls in town. They came from good families and had solid bodies that could plow the fields like oxen. Their families even agreed to forgo the standard marriage fees. One of the fathers promised to throw in two farming cows as part of the dowry. Not a bad deal, we joked. Cousin Tan laughed at them all and rejected their offers. He was our hope. We celebrated with him at a big banquet before he left. He encouraged my brother to take the plunge and cautioned me to concentrate on my major, make a reasonable study schedule, and persevere.

That night I sat in my room facing a tall stack of books; I assigned a time slot for each subject. In order to cram everything into a single day, every day, I had to get up at five and go to bed at ten-thirty, allowing only short breaks for lunch and dinner. No entertainment, no goofing off with friends, no daydreaming, only hard-core studying. My heart beat with the excitement of the challenge; I couldn't close my eyes. I tried to imagine what a college classroom looked like, occupied by sharp professors and leggy city girls wearing sexy skirts. The stars blinked from a clear sky and the moon shone through my window. I made up my mind. College was the only thing for me. I'd get out of this small-town hell-hole. If Tan could swing it, so could I.

Beijing. The word split into four parts that split again, winking at me like stars as I fell asleep.

Suddenly, school had a purpose. College was the goal, and ancient teachers like Mr. Du and the Peking Man paraded the street of Yellow Stone attracting many admiring looks and greetings. Only a few years before, shamed, they had walked the same street, wearing tall hats, with thick plaques hung around their necks on which their names were smudgily written in red ink. Their heads had been shaved and their hands tied behind their backs. Kids had thrown bricks at them and adults had spat in their faces. They were stinking intellectuals. Society had had no place for them then.

Mr. Du's former wife, who had left him a few years before, now begged to come back to him. Du didn't want her. He married a young teacher who fell under the magic spell of his mighty mathematical talents.

Genius and youthful beauty: the people of Yellow Stone could live with that. There were serious debates as to whether he would live longer or die sooner, given his new, energy-consuming marriage. Different schools of thought came to different conclusions. In the end he was the super-star teacher who had guessed correctly the answers to two big questions that had been on the national mathematics exam. He deserved to enjoy his new wife.

The Peking Man didn't have any problems with his

Peking woman, but luck also came his way. He was honored with Communist party membership. He called himself a fossil newly unearthed by the party. It was a mixed blessing he had difficulty accepting or rejecting. A cynical historian, he had his doubts about the party. But he also knew enough not to refuse such an offer. The Cultural Revolution could come back anytime and then he, the Peking Man, would be the one who had rejected party membership, thereby rejecting the party itself, maybe even rejecting the country. Then he would have to change his nationality or they might lock him away in some cage like they had the real Peking man.

They said he shed tears at the swearing ceremony. Many suspected they were tears of pain and suffering, not joy. Poor guy. As for my goldfish-eyed, wheezing English teacher, he retired after his wife became bedridden and incontinent. With him gone, the school didn't lose much. I could attest to that.

The finals for the fall semester loomed before us, and hardworking students were found lurking behind closed doors, hitting the books late into the night. And the students who boarded at school clutched their books and went off to find a quiet spot in which to study.

The school announced that teachers would use the results of the fall semester finals to help determine which majors the graduating students should concentrate on. I abandoned the leaking compartments of my ship, the science courses, and steered the good parts along the misty coast.

The teachers noticed I'd stopped going to science classes but didn't express concern.

I stopped going to Professor Wei's for two weeks and reviewed the subjects within the liberal arts field. I was up at five in the morning, taking my hurting body to bed at eleven. Teachers held review sessions for every subject. I skipped all the sessions, sequestering myself in my private spot in the wheat field outside the school's low wall, where I banged away at my books on my own.

The finals for the fall semester took three full days. At each test, I swaggered into the classroom empty-handed and chose a seat apart from everyone else. It was just me and the paper. I wanted the teachers to know that there was no possibility of cheating for this born-again student. My message was loud and clear; the teachers looked at me suspiciously. I scribbled quickly and answered all the questions in my best handwriting. Good presentation counted for a third of your score, Dad had cautioned me. I did the best I could. This was a defining moment: I was declaring my intention to join the race for college, and if anyone had any problems with it, I couldn't care less. I had been at the bottom before, crawling on my knees. Now I was limping along. Soon I would be running. I wanted the world to know that I wasn't born in order for someone to step on me.

I handed in the papers early. The teachers kept calm, their curiosity at bay, pretending not to look at me. As I left each classroom, I could feel their hands grabbing my papers and checking the answers. I knew they would be shaking their heads in amazement.

The results of the finals were significant, because the college entrance examinations were only seven months away. If you didn't make this one, you might as well go home, sharpen the farm tools, and register as a proud farmer for life, just in time for spring harvest.

I sweated through the semester finals, and the results blew me away.

On the public announcement wall on campus, my name

hovered at the top in every liberal arts subject. My proudest achievement was English. I scored 91 percent, putting me head to head with a guy they called the English Wizard, Cing, an apple-headed rival of mine since first grade.

Silently I thanked Professor Wei, my secret weapon.

Dia was busy trumpeting my victory like a pimp. He hung around the wall, smoking his thick one, shouting to anybody passing to look at the results, particularly mine. When the Head came by, Dia showed him my glories. The snobby science major sneered and told Dia that no one in the history of this lowly high school had ever dared dream of majoring in English. It was a major for the privileged city boys, not farm boys like us, who smelled like manure. It was an elegant major for high-class people: it had to do with the mysterious Western culture and capitalism; it had to do with America. The Head knew how to hurt a fragile soul. Dia spat at his feet, cursed like a sailor, and walked back to me like a loser.

"Is that true that no one in our school has ever made it as an English major?"

"It's true. Why?" I asked.

"You gotta make me proud. I was out there happy for you and the Head trashed me left and right. Now I'm totally busted up inside."

"Let me ask you, was there anyone in the history of this lowly school who ever played the violin before?" He blinked and cocked his head for a second before shaking it slowly. A broad grin spread across his sad face. "Right, you're the first one." He straightened up and hugged me violently.

"You could do it, man," Dia spat out excitedly, "and you gotta do it for me and the school. Then when you pack up and take the fabulous Fujiang-Beijing train, I'll load a shot-gun and shoot the Head right on his shining skull."

Mr. Ka, my new English teacher, was a dark-skinned young man with a head of feathery curls.

He summoned me into his office. "Congratulations," he said. "You finally woke up." He jerked his head violently. His curls were bothering him.

"I heard mixed things about you from some people, but it doesn't matter what they said anymore," he continued. "I like what I see now. You have potential." A brilliant opening line. He made a friend of me on the spot. It was us against them now.

"We have work to do to get you where you want to go." He was good with abstract terms. "I'll give you what I have and help you with what you need. Do you know what I mean?" I was clueless. I shifted in my seat and nodded am-biguously.

"First thing to push for is membership in the Young Com-munist League. I checked your record and it's pathetic. You weren't even a Little Red Guard in elementary school." Not the memory of my miserable elementary school again.

"Someone wronged you badly." He narrowed his eyes and looked out the window.

You bet it was wrong. It was criminal. I was the only one in the whole school who wasn't a Little Red Guard because I was from a Black family and was personally on the suspect list as a counterrevolutionary. I still had nightmares about it.

"It's time someone stood up for you. I'll get you the membership before you graduate. It'll enhance your chance of admission into a top-notch college like the one I went to. You don't want to be second-guessed on such a minor point, do you?"

"No, sir, and thank you, sir."

"No problem. I had the same conversation with Cing, another talented potential. You two are my only hopes for the year. I'll personally involve myself with your growth. Together we'll give it our best try." It brought to mind the pep talks from my Ping-Pong coach. The pep talks meant nothing, but they made you feel real good. A sort of national anthem in words.

Within days, a small red poster was pasted on the school wall. It attracted almost no attention. It stated that I was belatedly being given the glorious title of Little Red Guard and had been admitted into the Young Communist League. For a brief moment, I felt like the Peking Man, tickled by the emptiness of such a title. Communism had become a commodity with a price tag, its value plummeting a notch each time it was sold at a garage sale. Soon the membership would become a tradable commodity, one you could pick up for a penny with a cold drink thrown in.

I went to Mr. Ka's office to thank him. He slapped my shoulder and grabbed me with his strong hands.

"Congratulations, young comrade. You are the future of Communism." He spoiled the serious words by winking at me.

Professor Wei did the soprano thing when I told her the results. Her hands cupped beneath her chin and her silver head tilted to one side, she shook her head, speechless. She was in heaven. Her happiness for me was genuine. God bless her.

The school authorities regrouped the entire graduating

class, which amounted to just over five hundred students. They were now formed into six science and two liberal arts classes. S-One, which was what Science One was commonly called, consisted of the best science students and was where the Head and other snobs were. The school placed the best of its faculty in that class. The rest of the science classes were left to rot. Students held strikes against the school and threw rocks at S-One, and some snobs were even beaten for showing off their exclusivity. But the separation stayed.

L-One, or Liberal Arts One, also got the best Yellow Stone High had, which included the venerable Peking Man and an assortment of liberal arts buffs. It wasn't much, but it was all they had. Apple-headed Cing took the back seat on the right; I took the one on the left. Poor Dia was regrouped into L-Two, where he claimed to sleep through most of the mornings without being disturbed by the teachers. They didn't care. Students smoked in class and propped their feet on the desks. Teachers found warm, sunny spots and read novels.

Cousin Tan returned home for a visit. His hair was longer and he was wearing good shoes that would have been shiny if he'd bothered to polish them. His sunken cheeks had filled out, and he sported a few ballpoint pens lined up evenly in his jacket pocket. He crossed his legs, tapping his right foot languidly, his speech coming easily, filled with college jargon. He was on his spring break, with not a burden in the world. He sat in our living room, surrounded by my whole family.

"It's all good meat they serve there at AU." That stood for Amoy University.

"Even for breakfast?" I asked.

He nodded. "Pickled meat." What a luxury. I had never heard of such a thing, but I believed him.

My mouth watered and I had to swallow a few times at the delicious thought of meat steaming on a plate. My lofty goal of going to college vanished, and my desires became very basic. My whole body yearned for meat. Simmered, roasted, sautéed, boiled, fried, smoked, or pickled. What difference did it make? The bloody flesh tasted good whatever you did to it.

"We spent a whole long month on MT," he said casually.

The whole family shrugged. MT? What was that? Meat Truck? "Military Training, that is, for all AU students," Cousin Tan explained. "Look at my hands." He stretched out his hands for us to see.

"They're all callused now. See how hard the rifles have made them." *It wasn't AU or MT that made his hands rough,* I thought. *It was FW, Farm Work.*

"I heard you are preparing for an English major," he said, fingering a callus on his right hand.

"Yeah, what do you think?" Mom had urged me to seek his advice; now I was all ears.

"How should I say it?" He recrossed his legs and leaned back. "I've met some English majors at AU. They were all rich kids from the large city of Fuzhou and, of course, Amoy. You know, the kind that wear expensive clothes and watches, ride fancy bikes, and have lots of spending money. They're artistic and romantic." His eyes narrowed as if he were staring at a mirage, close but untouchable. "There was one pretty, slender girl, jeans and all, who was so talented she could speak English more fluently than some of the teachers there. She was from HK, you know." Hong Kong. "I wouldn't try for English. You have all the disadvantages. Those guys all have big, foreign tape recorders complete with American language tapes. Have you seen a recorder before?" He shook his head. "Of course not." I still didn't believe it was humanly possible to preserve the sound of a human voice once it had spoken. It was like trying to gather water once it had spilled.

"Those guys have beautiful, perfect accents. It's talent. You have to be artistic and musical. I don't think anyone at YSH [Yellow Stone High] could teach you that. And even if they could, we would be stuck, given our thick lips and slow tongues. If I were you, I would consider something else, maybe agricultural management."

I saw my dad lose interest in talking to this new city man. He rolled a thick one and offered it to my cousin. I knew Dad was being funny. He should know that they wouldn't do thick ones on the AU campus.

Cousin Tan refused it, pulled out a Wing cigarette, and offered one to Dad and my brother.

"What is it?" Dad asked.

"Oh, it's the most popular brand on campus. Even the chairman of my department at AU smokes these."

Dad shook his head violently from side to side, like a Yellow Stone farmer. "Not my type. It's too light, it'll make me sneeze." He broke the cigarette in half and dropped it on the floor. "Why don't you stay for lunch?" Dad's way of saying good-bye. Mom frowned warningly at him.

"No, no. I have to go to Putien to see some AU classmates, you know." Sure, we knew. Socializing. It was a part of high society. We had no meat for lunch, in any case. We watched him comb his longish hair with his hands and walk with a straight back down the narrow street of Yellow Stone, greeting people with a wave of his hand like a victorious Napoleon.

I retreated to my room after he had left, taking two hours

to rebuild the spirit he had so gently and carelessly dashed. But no matter how tacky he had become, I still liked it better than seeing him locked up in his attic. He had the freedom to vent his airs now. That was what it was all about. I renewed my determination, wanting to be in his shoes, if not necessarily like him.

"Do you still want to pursue the English major?" Dad asked me later.

"Yes, even more so."

"Why?"

"Because I think they've got a bunch of losers and playboys at AU. I'm not afraid of city folks. They're wimpy, I'm tough. They already have everything without college. I don't. I'll work my butt off and beat every one of those pompous spoiled brats. Don't you think I can do it?"

Dad smiled and nodded confidently. He blew a perfect smoke ring.

I caught it with my index finger, cutting it in half.

TWENTY

造

Firecrackers filled Yellow Stone's narrow street with thick smoke. It was Chinese New Year again. Farming was halted and half the town was into serious gambling. The well-off smoked their Flying Horses and bet with cash; the stingy made do with grains or animals as bets; and the desperate smoked their thick handmade rolls and even put their wives on the betting table.

A villager fifteen miles west of Yellow Stone was heard to have lost his wife twelve times at one sitting. When she got word, she drove him out of their house and had the commune arrest him, disclaiming her association with such a shameless loser.

When I'd eaten the noodles that were traditionally served as the first meal of the year, and after spending the kowtow money on five packs of Flying Horse at Liang's black market, I headed for Yi's old workshop.

The gang was already there. They roughed up my hair and

pinched my ears and nose, paying me back for all the times I had been too busy for them. I loved these guys. They were always the same: gruff, sincere, and caring in their own very charming way. When they felt jealous or neglected, they shouted at me and slapped my head; then their irritation was over. Like the Dong Jing, full to its brim with pure rainwater, their hearts were generous with love.

"Hey, you look pale and weak. What's the matter with you, college man?" Mo Gong made the welcome speech for the gang. Sen, Yi, and Siang searched my coat pockets, split up the cigarettes, and laughingly enjoyed their first good smoke of the year.

"I brought these for you guys because I wanted to apologize for all the neglect."

"Shut up and have one yourself." Sen threw me a pack of Wing cigarettes with filters. I lit one. It felt good to be back.

Sen patted my shoulder and sat next to me on Yi's old work stool. "Brother, you missed out on a helluva lot of fun when you were hittin' those books."

"What the hell have you guys been doing?" I asked.

"Take a look." Mo Gong threw a thick heap of money on the bench and nodded. It was supposed to mean something to me. I had never seen that much money before. The butcher next door carried a wad to the commune bank at the end of every day, but this neatly stacked pile was twice as thick.

"Where did you get it? Did you steal it?" I couldn't believe my eyes.

The four gave me another roughing up and pinched my ears and nose again. I struggled free before any more damage could be done. They all smiled the same Buddha smile, silent and mysterious.

"We went to Yi's city for ten days and won it," Sen said.

"How?" I asked.

"Well, we set up two gambling tables in a rented hut near Yi's factory. Half of Yi's colleagues came, just for the entertainment. Those rich city folks! We robbed them raw and stole them blind. Yi played stranger, and we three ran the two tables. Before word got out, we moved, and here we are. Nine hundred and thirty yuan!" Sen exclaimed.

"The money is yours, too. You're still our brother. We'll use it as seed money to gamble some more, and soon we'll all be rich and maybe buy ourselves some wives," Mo Gong said, lights dancing in his eyes. At the end of the sentence, he winked. Money first, then a wife. It was Mo Gong being totally honest about his worldly outlook.

I felt touched by their inclusion of me. The brother thing still caused a tightening in my gut. We were bound by our sworn allegiance, but when money came into it, things changed somehow. I felt uncomfortable. We were meant to stick together in friendship and love, not for money. No one had inserted any clause about money. Ours was a spiritual alliance, not a financial one.

Something about them had changed. These guys were no longer kids. They had all begun to wear rough beards. Their voices were deeper and huskier. They were grown-ups with grown-up desires and ideas. They had seen the city and gambled there with the big guys.

Now there was this pot of money. Who knew what was next? Maybe the cops were after them.

"Are you sure this money is clean?" I asked, stern-faced.

"Smug little rascal." Mo Gong grabbed my neck and planted a wet kiss on my forehead. "Don't worry about a thing. Money is always clean." He picked up the stack and planted a kiss on that, too. "We're rich. Let's hit the fields. The losers are waiting for us to wipe them out."

"This time we're the big guys," Sen said. "Only big hands are welcome from now on. The penny business is over. Da, you come with us, even if it's just for a day or two; then you can go back to your studies."

"You have to come. Just spend some time with us, okay?" Siang said.

"And we've got some love stories for you to hear." The temptation was high. It was New Year's Day. No one could say anything about my taking a day off from my studies. I deserved it. Four pairs of eyes were watching me, waiting for me.

I bit my lips. "I really need to study every night to make it to college, I swear. I'd love to come with you and wipe them out, or even just be with you guys and boast, but I really can't go." It was the pact I had made with my family and Buddha. I had better stick to it.

There was disappointment in their eyes.

Sen was a man of reason. "Well, we're all grown up now. If you gotta do it, then go do it. Let's have a drink tonight, though."

"I'll be here with all the food you can eat. You guys go make big money, and we'll celebrate tonight."

"You better be hitting the books or else I'll crack your skull," Mo Gong threatened affectionately. He would have made a great law enforcement officer.

Yi and Siang both kicked my behind as I left them.

On my way home, I thought about them and the money. Things used to be simpler. There had been no college to dream about, and my friends had just been lightweight neighborhood hooligans, walking their beat on the street of

Yellow Stone. A puff of smoke could make them content, and a good joke could last for days. Tobacco had been sweet and liquor charming. Now I was turning down their offer of adventure to hit my tedious books, while they headed out on a mission to clean out the whole town. The thought wedged in the middle of my heart. I sighed as I entered our house and crept into my room, where my books were waiting patiently for me. I closed my eyes before opening the first book to study the first item on the agenda for the day.

There was peace within me. The excitement of the new year belonged out there, on the street of Yellow Stone.

Dad had brewed a tall pot of strong tea. He sat comfortably in his old cane chair with his feet on a stool. The well-wishers of the New Year had gone home. It was quiet family time. My brother sat in the corner lighting a cigarette while Dad poured a cup of steaming tea for him and filled another for me.

"It's New Year's Day and we have made a new decision about your brother," Dad said to me. "He is going to take time off and start preparing for the college exam. What do you think?" Dad sounded confident. Once he had made a decision, he considered that eighty percent of the job was done. He had faith that if he believed in us, we could swim the ocean and climb mountains. No hurdle was too high to leap, no glory too lofty to obtain.

I looked at my brother, who was smoking quietly, then at my dad.

"Dad, why didn't I hear about it sooner? I'll go make room for him in my study; I know I'll learn a lot from him."

Pleased with my response, Dad rolled up his sleeves. "Now, here is the strategy for you two. Da, you are still fresh. You're going to help your brother. You'll make a schedule and study together." I was surprised. Jin, who was two sisters away from me, had been in first grade when I was still crawling around in my diapers fighting for food with the chickens in the courtyard. Now I was to help him. My heart beat with pride. With a little hard work and a bit of determination, I had won my dad's respect.

"That will be great," I said, turning to my brother. "I have all the books."

"I'm not really sure about college; I've been away from books for too long." Jin sounded pessimistic. He had always been my opposite in many ways. He was calm and wise, never one to take center stage. When it came to a major decision, we always had to push and shove him a little. I hoped for victory, while he worried about failure.

"You can do it," Dad told Jin. "You were the math wizard of your class in junior high. You will devote your time to learning the other subjects over the next seven months. Don't worry, son, I feel lucky this year.

"Son, this is the chance of a lifetime," he went on, turning to me. "I thought you guys would never have the opportunity to dream about college. Now Mao has gone west and you're given a chance to try. The Chen men have never been known for lack of talent, only for lack of opportunity."

He turned again to my brother, lit another cigarette for him, and said, "Jin, you have the advantage of being more mature. Da, you have the energy. Work together like brothers should, make up for the disadvantages, and both of you will win this time. All you need to do is work hard. Jin, if you as a teenager could farm like an adult to support this family, then there is no college, I mean no college under the sun, that should be too hard for you to get into. We are behind you all the way. And you, Da, have no reason to even consider anything other than your first choice of college. Beijing. Shanghai. Anywhere your heart belongs.

"Young men, you don't know how lucky you are. Look at your sisters. They weren't even allowed to finish elementary school." Dad ended his speech, his eyes fiery. The conversation had turned from father-son chitchat into an admiral's final order. *The enemy is at the front door. Now go get them, sons.*

Jin quietly put out his cigarette and said to me, "Tomorrow, wake me when you get up. Let me get a feel of what's going on; then we'll sit down and talk. Make me work hard if you see me slack off, little brother. We'll work together."

"Sure thing."

Dad filled our cups again and symbolically drank his in one gulp. He had said enough. Now it was up to us.

"Bottoms up." I toasted my brother and rose to leave. When I pushed the door open, Mom was right behind it and had probably been listening to the whole conversation.

I climbed the stairs to my room and sat down at my desk, which was covered with piles of books. The sense of a sacred mission swept through my heart. Just before this pep talk, college had been a young man's romantic ideal. Now it was a reality full of emotions. If I failed, I failed the whole family all the way back to our earliest ancestor, whose tombstone had long ago become sand. If I succeeded, the family's ship would sail again. It was about pride, humiliation, revenge, dignity, and vindication of the family name.

I compiled two lists. One was a checklist of everything my brother needed to do to catch up with me. The other was my own list of dos and don'ts, a sort of New Year's resolution. On it were no movies, no plays, no sports, no more time off until after the Big One. Tonight would be my last night out with my friends.

A popular local melody was being badly distorted by a whistler just below my window. The nightingale was Siang, the designated messenger from the gang.

I closed my book, went to the kitchen, and picked up the food basket Mom had prepared for my friends. When I had asked her for the food, I had promised her that it was my last night out with them, that from now on, I would shut my door and bury my head in my books.

"What a terrible whistler," Mom said. "Why don't they come in?"

"Because they're afraid of you."

"Why?"

"Because you're a good person," I replied.

"How strange."

"Well, my friends aren't afraid of bad people, they deal with them all day long and beat them up all the time. But when they meet a good person like you, they don't know what to do. They turn shy and stay in the dark." Mom shook her head and wiped her hands on her apron.

When I pushed the door open at Yi's, no one jumped out to throw me to the floor or pinch my neck. It was quiet. Four heads, a cloud of smoke rising above them, slumped between legs.

"Hey, brothers, the food is here. Why is everyone so quiet?"

"We lost half our money," Sen said in a low voice. His eyebrows were locked together, a hairy mess.

"How?" My heart dropped. Five hundred yuan gone like the wind. "That's impossible. You guys are the quickest hands north of the equator and east of the Western world." I shook Mo Gong's fuzzy head. His neck was boneless, like a rubber pipe. The picture of prosperity only hours ago, he was now a deflated balloon.

"We were doing fine at the beginning, wiping out people like a typhoon. I mean big hands. Then someone sneaked from the fields and reported us to the commune. They sent in a battalion and cleaned our pockets. Good thing we made for the sugarcane—that's why we're not sitting stinking in the commune jail."

"But the police got our names," Siang said. "It's only a matter of hours before they come and knock at our door."

"What? Who reported it?" I asked.

"Some guy from another village. We'll take care of him sooner or later."

"So let's eat first and then run," I said.

"I don't think we have time to eat. But we need some money; we're broke," Sen said.

"What about the other half of the money?" I asked.

"In the field. We buried it. We'll get it later. Now ain't a good time," Sen replied.

"Here." I dug into my pocket and took out about ten yuan. "Not much, but take this for now."

"That's a lotta money," Yi said.

"Don't worry. I have no place to spend it," I said, pushing the money into Sen's hands. He took it slowly.

"Thanks, Da, you're a real pal. We'll borrow it," he said, his head low.

"It's nothing, and it's not enough for you guys. Hey, if you wait, I could go home and get some more." I was thinking of borrowing from my brother.

"No, no, we're leaving now," Sen said.

"Do you have to?" All four heads nodded in unison.

"Listen, if we go now, we'll be in Putien in a few hours. We'll stay at Yi's and make another living there. If we don't, it'll be jail time."

"Eat the food up, please, or you'll be hungry." I opened the basket.

The smells of fried fish, roasted pork, noodles, and New Year's rice cakes permeated the room and opened their eyes.

"Here, use your hands. Eat." Four pairs of hands fought for the juiciest pieces. Soon Mo Gong was licking the bottom of the meat plate and Siang was burping. Sen wiped his greasy hands on his hair, a habit he had since he was young, and Yi picked his teeth. A perfect last supper.

The four of them touched me with their greasy hands before leaving. Sen whispered to me, "Work hard, college man. Make us proud." I carried the empty basket home, feeling like a fugitive myself. My friends had vanished into the darkness. All I could hear was the clanking of the old bike.

TWENTY-ONE

The first day back from the New Year's break, Dia sported a brand-new army green Mao jacket. One of the pockets was already missing a button. He stood outside our door and looked as dopey as a bridegroom.

"Hey, happy New Year, and how in the world did you make the girl marry you?" I faked a frown and crossed my arms across my chest.

Dia rubbed his reddened face. "This thing?" His hands smoothed the wrinkles on his jacket. "Mom made it for my elder brother and the stupid guy washed it in boiling water. It shrank two sizes. Now I gotta wear it. I took the button off to look more casual."

We chose the narrow path between two green wheat fields, still wet from the melting frost. The morning sun gleamed through the fog. The trees, road, and endless fields looked like an Impressionist painting, fuzzy.

"I feel ashamed walking beside you, you know," Dia suddenly said.

"Why?"

"I heard that you locked yourself up in your room and banged your head against the wall studying, and that you didn't even take New Year's Day off. You didn't, did you, you son-of-a-gun?"

"That was pure rumor. I had a great time this holiday."

"Not true. I have my source."

"I wouldn't rely on it entirely," I teased him.

"Wait." Dia ran in front of me. "I heard something you might wanna hear."

"What?"

"About your friends."

"What about them?"

"You haven't heard anything?"

"No, I haven't heard from them since they skipped town on New Year's."

"Don't pull my leg." Dia stopped me in the middle of the narrow road. His small eyes radiated sincerity.

"I swear to Buddha," I said. "Tell me what you heard."

"Okay, here's a clue. Money."

"Money? What money are you talking about?" My heart sank. Even Dia knew about their fortune.

"You sure you don't know anything about this? Okay, the rumor out there had it that Siang stole about a thousand yuan from the commune's shoe factory his father runs. That's why he's been hiding out with his friends." The news hit me like a fist. Siang, a thief? On the run? I recalled the glee on my friends' faces on New Year's Day. They had been so full of joy.

That one thousand yuan had to have been money they'd won honestly.

Siang wouldn't steal. My sworn friends wouldn't lie to me about where they had gotten the fortune. It hadn't been in their eyes. There had been no fear. It was money that had come from bravery and their ability to take a calculated risk at the gambling table.

"You don't believe me, do you?" Dia asked.

"No, I don't. They told me a different story."

"What? They told you about the money?"

I realized my slip of the tongue. "Forget it, Dia. We didn't have this conversation, okay?"

"Hey, slow down. I'm your best friend. Trust me. The commune is investigating the whole thing now and they can't prove whether Siang really has the money that he was accused of stealing."

Holy shit, I could have given the truth away. I was glad I was only talking to Dia, someone in whom I could confide my darkest secrets. "What else did you hear?"

"That he stole the money to gamble, but there's another rumor that the shoe factory's one thousand yuan might have been stolen by its bookkeeper or someone from the inside. Someone knew that Siang was in possession of a fortune and framed him. He was easy pickings. You know he hangs around the shoe factory and is good friends with the treasurer."

My heart sank lower. There was a scheme out there to frame and ruin Siang and his friends, and possibly me. "Did you hear anything about me being involved in any way?"

"No, everyone knows you're a born-again good guy who was recently honored with the Young Communist League title in school. You've been making quite a name as being a top contender for college."

"How does your small village know so much about the things happening here?"

"My neighbor, the baldy. Remember, I told you about him. He's the head of the commune's militia command. He was drunk last night, boasting to my dad. I got the whole scoop. He's heading the investigation."

"What's he doing now?"

"Nothing concerning you," he told me. "Relax." I had never felt so relieved. I prayed a quiet thank-you to Buddha that I hadn't followed them to the fields to gamble on New Year's Day. I could easily have been implicated. Buddha had been watching over me.

A dark shadow clouded my mood. My friends were in trouble. I should do something about it, but I didn't have a clue what. I truly believed that they had gone to Putien and cleaned Yi's colleagues out. They were self-made rich men, unjustly put on a short list of suspects. It would have been easy. They were social outcasts. Someone had probably known about their money, swiped the cash from the shoe factory, and laid the crime on them, just in time to get away clean. The whole town would believe it was Siang, of course. It was the holidays, gambling time, and he just happened to be back in town on the day the crime occurred. He probably went to see his dad at work and someone saw him and heard about the money they had won in Putien. Bingo. What better motive, what better timing!

Inside the school, the Head walked by us with his nose up in the air. He sported a new jacket, as well as a new hat for his formidable pate. He hurried by, sneering and ignoring us as if we were a couple of stinking bugs he wouldn't mind stepping on and grinding to death.

"That guy annoys the heck out of me," I said to Dia.

"My feeling exactly. Watch this." Dia cleared his throat and shouted, "Hey, Head, there's bird droppings on your new hat." The Head stopped without turning around. He knew where the voice came from. He thought for a second, then took off his new wool hat and checked the top quickly.

"Oops, I lied." Dia laughed.

"You little rat." The Head was angry. He rolled up his sleeves and walked up to Dia, who stood his ground.

I inserted myself between them and said, "There's no reason to get angry here. Dia just wanted to see your head, that's all. It's a joke. Can't you take a joke, big boy?"

"I can take a joke, but not from you two losers." The Head gritted his teeth.

"Hey, watch your mouth." I felt like shaking the guy. From the corner of my eye I saw Dia reaching into his bag, ready to do some serious damage to the self-proclaimed top intellectual of Yellow Stone High. I quickly put my hand on his arm.

"Why are you wasting your time in school?" the Head said. "You guys belong in the fields. There's no future for you two in school."

"Says who? You?" I stepped closer.

"Says everyone. Haven't you heard? Liberal arts is just a dumping ground for waste like you guys. Don't think a few good scores will get you into college. No way."

My anger was reaching its peak. You could insult my looks, my character, and my honor, but no one was allowed to tear apart my dream. I pulled back my right arm, ready to shove my fist down his throat. This time Dia dragged me back.

"Hey, Head, let me tell you something. This man"—Dia pointed at me—"is gonna be an English major at a top college in Beijing, while you, the engineering major, will end up in a corner of this freezing country, spending your miserable life sawing lumber in the snow. And you're gonna get so lonely, you're gonna start thinking about a sheep while this man will be the translator for the Minister of Foreign Affairs, touring the beautiful Western world. Wake up, Head, and think."

My anger subsided at Dia's rousing speech.

"In your dreams." The Head put back his hat and walked off proudly.

Dia and I looked at each other and laughed. There was a reason why we liked each other. We worked well together, unrehearsed.

"How do you come up with stuff like that?" I asked Dia.

"Well, that's what I think is gonna happen to you, man. Don't disappoint me. Work your bony butt off if you have to and do honor to our friendship. I have high hopes for you and low expectations for that creep. I don't get it. How can such a big head be so stupid? I think the best thing for him to do would be to hand over his head to some scientist, who can study it and find out what's wrong with it. That would be his biggest contribution to science." We had another good laugh.

The classroom was half full when I came in. There had been some changes. The broken windows were fixed and the wall was repainted with rough white paint. There was a large slogan about studying hard, a quote from the dead Chairman Mao. Students buried their heads in their books. Some stuck their heads out of the window and puffed their tobacco rolls. There was a sense of seriousness that hadn't been there before. A fellow was actually reading an English lesson out loud.

Only a year ago, his teeth would have been knocked out for doing that.

I sat in my old seat, in the corner of the last row. The corner was no longer for the convenience of jumping out the window whenever I felt like it. It was an island. I felt safe here; I could survey everything and everyone, yet no one could see me.

It was ironic to bring Mao into this drive for intellectual excellence. If Mao had known what his Little Red Guards were doing, he would have howled like a lonely wolf in his icy coffin and cried his smoke-ridden lungs out. Mao, the dictator, had been the friend of the devils. He had wanted China in perpetual turmoil so that he could rule forever. He'd had a simple philosophy: peace and leisure bred unrest and resentment against leaders, while a sense of crisis strengthened his own leadership.

That was why, ever since the Communists took over in 1949, Mao hadn't stopped making fake smoke over fake fires. One political movement had followed another. And strewn down his long path lay the bones of millions of angry ghosts. He hadn't cared about the young generation, whom he had ordered to walk out of school and into the countryside to get reeducated by the poor farmers in their muddy fields. He had simply wanted them to be ignorant so that they wouldn't be aware of what a fiend he really was.

Young people loved it. Since the big guy didn't want them in school, they packed up and moved to the countryside by the millions, singing the Red Guard songs and waving their Little Red Books. But soon they found that all they could learn from farmers was backbreaking labor and antiquated farming techniques dating back thousands of years. So they started insulting the farmers and stealing their daughters and stopped going to work. All day long the youngsters smoked, drank, gambled, and fell in love. There was nothing else out there to do.

The lonely countryside became their trap. They roamed around the hills, but it was too late to move back to the cities they had come from, because of China's population control system. A city person could easily give up his registration to move downward into the country, but not vice versa. They cried, and some committed suicide. Now they understood what their leader, Mao, had meant by finding your roots in the countryside. He had meant it literally. *Go marry someone there, breed a litter of ignorant farmers, and never come back to the city to bother me again.*

At eight sharp the old bellman wobbled to the bronze bell that hung under an old pine tree. The sound of the bell echoed far and wide. In the school hallway, the Peking Man snuffed out his cigarette and shuffled into our classroom. He smiled like a gorilla at the new slogan on the wall. He tried hard for a few seconds to conceal his laughter, but his thin lips were unable to cover his big teeth.

"Who put it there?" Peking Man asked. "Is that a joke or something?" The class was very quiet.

"When Mao said study hard, I don't think he meant the kind of stuff we're studying now," he stuttered. "You should know that he was referring to his Little Red Book, but I doubt any college would give you credit for that." The whole class rocked with laughter. Only Peking Man could open the first class of the year that way. What he said was brave, because Mao's ghosts still haunted the nation, but Peking Man was fearless and angry. He had been beaten and sent to labor camps not too long ago.

He snapped his fingers and the class calmed down. "About learning history, let me tell you a story." We were all ears.

"When I was at the university, I roomed with a medical student. Every night before going to sleep, the guy stuck his hand into a wooden box under his bed and mumbled things. Day in and day out. Finally, I couldn't contain my curiosity and I asked him what he was doing. You know what he said? He had a whole collection of human bones in that box. He was trying to develop a feel for the bones blindfolded, because he wanted to be a good doctor.

"What are the bones of history?" Peking Man paused and looked at us.

"From that day on, I did the same thing with all the historical facts: dates and names of the dynasties, all the important little things in the study of history. I had flash cards, stacks of them, under my bed next to my stinking shoes. Before we turned out the lights, he would be busy with his bones, and I with my cards. We had a grand time. We both graduated with honors."

Peking Man didn't ask us to do the same thing; he simply inspired and challenged us to follow in his footsteps. He was the perfect teacher for us to follow. His hairy chest, long limbs, formidable face, and that mountain of a jaw all attested to a man who knew the past well.

"Now, I heard that you guys are going to take the liberal arts examination. We don't have a lot of time left. Thousands of years of history have to be learned and relearned. I am here to guide you, but you have to do the rowing. Do you have any special requests before I begin?"

"How many questions did you guess right on the last national history examination?" one boy asked.

My question exactly.

"I would say I guessed them all, because I taught them all."

"No. I meant in the final days, when you gave your cram session," the boy persisted.

"Oh, that. Three out of the five essay questions. I gave my last graduating class the exact answers two days before the test. I considered it my gift to them. The smart ones went home and committed them to memory, and they came out of the test smiling from ear to ear." Another point driven home. *Thou shalt heed my words.* Peking Man had the mentality of a god, and we were brought down on our knees in the presence of his achievement.

"But," he said, "my guessing is just a bonus. Sometimes I guess correctly, other times I don't. You need to go home and chew up this thick volume." He waved his textbook as if it were scripture. "Digest this and make it become part of you. Every word in here, every fact, is a building block to your dream of a college degree. Young people like you belong there." His eyes swept across me, and my heart warmed up ten degrees. "Remember, for the next few months you have to sleep, eat, walk, and talk with these books. And you students who are behind, you had better dream about them as well."

During the winter holiday, I had finished my history studies. They included Chinese ancient history, world history, and the stupid history of the Communist party. The subjects were contained in a thick volume of one thousand pages. In the beginning, I had been stunned by how many dynasties China had. The names of all the emperors and their successors piled up like endless waves of the Dong Jing River.

Gradually, I developed a method of study. I arranged the dynasties into a series of charts, a family tree, and gave them funny names, like those I used to give to my dogs, chickens, and ducks. I carried the charts with me at all times and reviewed them again and again, even when I went to the bathroom.

Every minute was put to good use in my schedule.

TWENTY-TWO

造

Every morning I rose with the sun. Then I shuffled to my brother's room and woke him up. I went through our backyard, opened the squeaky door, trotted down the steps to the river, and squatted by the clear, cool water to check my reflection. I splashed my face with water and wiped it with my sleeves. Six hours of sleep every day. I needed a lot of cold water to keep my eyes open.

It was already late April. The smell of summer was pungent everywhere. Our backyard was a colorful garden with red roses, yellow gagai blossoms, and white lilies. Mom had planted some lima beans, which had flourished in the most imaginative way and now crawled overhead along the wood frames of the doors and windows. I found a spot beneath the thick leaves, away from the scorching sun, placed my favorite bamboo chair there, and munched on some bean pods as the gentle breeze ruffled my hair.

I started by tackling political studies, the most boring of

the five subjects required in the big exam. It was all about the twisted philosophy of the Communist party. Some of the theories were so involved, they sounded like sophistry at best, and that was what they were.

It was like a carpet-cleaning salesman raving about this great revolution taking place in the carpet-cleaning industry, when actually none existed. And the machine he was trying to sell you wasn't one bit as good as what he claimed. It was tedious self-promotion, mixed with a little bit of lying. Many times I wanted to throw the book into the river. What was this? Marxism combined with Mao's superior thoughts? It was simply some foreign garbage, stir-fried with local flavor until it became a dish called Communism, Chinese style. Moo goo gai pan with ketchup.

Some of the questions and explanations given were so far-fetched, I felt like spitting. Like why in the beginning of the revolution Mao had ordered his armies into the countryside instead of starting a revolt in the big city. The book said Mao was applying Marxism to China's unique circumstances. That was bull. Mao was just running for his life.

He hadn't even had time to wipe his ass. The Nationalist army was after his head and he'd had to flee into the woods. There had been no Marxism in his mind at that time.

I almost puked as I read a whole chapter talking about the virtue of Mao's one-liner "True knowledge comes from practice." Yeah, right.

Well, he'd had plenty of practice, starting with dumping his ugly country-bumpkin first wife and crawling into bed with a chic Shanghai actress, while his army was chewing tree roots and getting their butts frozen in northern Shanghai, a hiding spot in which they were eventually able to revive.

But reality was reality. Political studies stayed, accounting for one fifth of the exam's total 500 points. I swallowed the sawdust and tried to keep my sentiments to a minimum.

After three months of intensive work, Jin was making amazing headway. I fed him all that I had and gave him my best guidance. He didn't need much help. Neither did he need any motivational pep talk.

While we studied, our three sisters toiled under the sun, taking over the workload for my brother. Each day, they came back sweaty and exhausted. My brother and I would come to the door to greet and thank them. They would just smile and ask us how much we had studied that day. We would tell them, and they would be happy for us. There were such hope and caring in their eyes. Brother Jin couldn't wait to jump back into farming as soon as the tests were over. He couldn't stand the thought that someone else was bearing his load for him. He knew how grueling the summer heat was, how sore your back could get, and that no matter how callused your hands were, cutting the rice with the ancient, blunt sickles gave you raw, open blisters every year. It was life at Yellow Stone we were trying to escape from.

After a light breakfast—three bowls of rice porridge for Jin and two for me—we studied geology and history together at a long table in the living room, facing the lush garden. We drew history charts on our makeshift blackboard, and more were spread all over the floor. We examined every detail of China's long history and pored over every exotic city in the world.

Jin sometimes offered me a cigarette during our five-minute afternoon break as we talked about our dreams and desires. His were practical and comfortable, while mine were whimsical and somewhat far-fetched. He wanted to go to a solid college with a good economics department near home, become a manager of a company, marry a pretty girl with a solid temperament, and raise a family. I wanted to go to Beijing, the pearl of China, which was a fifty-hour train ride from home, and study English. From there, the sky was the limit.

Mom would bring in our lunches, rice with some meat soup. I knew that we didn't have any money, so I asked Mom where the money to buy the meat came from. She was quiet for a bit, then said we needed nutrition to study, that I was not to worry, just to continue the good work. I knew that our family was probably piling up loans just to feed our two nonperforming mouths. Jin and I talked, and we decided to tell Mom to stop doing it. It was getting a little too luxurious for us. We just wanted simple soup made with vegetables from our garden, and a lot of rice. April was when the green couldn't meet the yellow, the time right before harvest when the food from the last harvest was about to run out. And we didn't know where Mom got all that long-grain white rice. By then we should have been eating just cheap yams three times a day, but that was something we didn't want to concern ourselves about at the moment.

I decided a lot of time could be saved by not going to school anymore. Everything was in the books. By April, most of the real teaching had been accomplished.

Jin and I stopped talking about dreams and instead tested each other on everything, the more detailed the better. We became so involved that when we took a bathroom break at the same time, we still tested each other through the thin partition separating our stalls. Every minute counted.

Soon we began to lengthen our days by two hours, adding an hour before sunrise and an hour in the evening. We lived on four hours of sleep. Our appetites diminished. Dad was concerned and gave us a brief lecture. We shrugged it off. The exam was only a couple of weeks away. What more harm could such a short time do? When Jin was tired, he stared into the empty space before him, deep in thought. His cheeks were sunken, his face was wan, and he'd grown an unruly beard. Each time I took my eyes off my book and stole a glance at him, my heart went out to him. He was a man consumed by his quest for the only way out of this hell-hole. He wanted only to give it one try. If he failed, he was going to burn those books and be a farmer forever. Each minute of his time was precious. I prayed silently for us every night before going to sleep, even on my most exhausting days.

We smiled and encouraged each other. I had never felt closer to Jin, nor he to me. We were a couple of marathon runners, each taking inspiration from the other. We kept saying to each other that, yes, we were nearing the finish line: hurry, hurry, or it would be forever too late.

Immediately after the Cultural Revolution ended, going to college suddenly became the rage. The radio talked about young heroes who had overcome severe difficulties and had made it to prestigious colleges. Heroism, glamour, money, and cushy jobs awaited those who crossed the threshold. A college education was money in the bank—and getting there was as rare as hitting all six numbers in the lottery.

In China, from the moment you were admitted into a college, no matter how low-level it was, your life would be totally taken care of by the government. There was no tuition to pay. They gave you the train ticket, a food stipend of thirty-six *jin* (about thirty-three pounds) of rice a month, a bed, all the books you needed, and a guaranteed job—a prestigious white-collar job. It was the best college deal in the whole world.

I drew a flag in red ink on the calendar for each of the three examination days in July. Each day, as I looked at the flags, I felt a lump in my throat. My blood would begin to boil, my heart would race, and my exhaustion would vanish as my energy returned. I would rush back to my books and read for a few more hours.

Finally, the big exam was only ten days away. Jin began to have difficulty sleeping. No matter how early he got up and how hard he studied, he still couldn't find peace. He would stare at the top of the mosquito net and listen to the mosquitoes hum their war songs. Dad had to find some sleeping pills to help calm him down. There were times when Jin would simply sit quietly, staring at his book, his eyes unmoving, thinking and thinking. I knew the pressure he was feeling.

He began to claim he couldn't remember anything. I made him some tea and told him that we were not going to waste all the work we'd done. We hadn't slept enough, had seen no friends, and had hardly been outside the house in weeks. Finally, I tested him on a few tough questions and he answered them beautifully. I slapped him on the back and he returned to his studies. At this point, we were bound together like a couple of soldiers in battle. My words meant more to him than anyone else's.

In the back of my own mind, however, there was always the fear of opening the exam paper and not knowing any of the answers. I had nightmares about my mind going blank. I woke up sweating and shaking.

TWENTY-THREE

As the sacred days slowly approached, the atmosphere in our household changed. Mom prayed a little harder and got up earlier to say longer prayers. Meals were more lavish. There was always meat on the table, just for Jin and me. We no longer argued with Mom about this unjust inequality among family members; we simply shoveled the food down and returned to our studies. Our sisters lowered their voices when they talked and walked past our rooms quietly. But the biggest change was in Dad. He actually bought some Flying Horses and slipped them into my room late at night. No words were needed. He badly wanted me to succeed.

Two days before the exam, the whole town of Yellow Stone gathered to gossip and watch the candidates. Every third family had someone taking the exam. Few public events mattered as much to the townspeople. A militiaman from the commune paraded through the street with a loud-speaker, shouting about the virtues of the exam and yelling encouragement. "Don't panic, be brave, have a strong heart, and be prepared for both failure and success."

The slogans roared through the speakers, which had been mounted on the front of a muddy tractor. People listened quietly as the tractor drove noisily by. It was wartime, and the young people were going out to do battle.

Food vendors loaded up their supplies and rented spaces near the test sites. Yellow Stone's high school and elementary school, where some of the tests would be held, were swept, mopped, and dusted by hundreds of temporary workers. The desks were all numbered, and schoolteachers were called back from their breaks to be monitors. The commune had several thousand exam applicants, all of whom were going to crowd into the town of Yellow Stone, the seat of higher learning, and take the tests that would determine their futures. Word was out that Peking Man was going to give his final predictions on the history questions. Since the entrance to the school was sealed, he would hold court in the commune's auditorium. His moment of glory had finally arrived. The site of much political significance was turned into his shrine.

I strolled along the street for the first time in months and headed for the commune. Jin felt ashamed to be among the younger crowd. He stayed at home and took a nap. Only the graduates of Yellow Stone High were allowed in. Hundreds more stood outside the hall. Peking Man had set the rules; he was a tribal type, loyal to his own kind and nasty to all others.

We sat on the crowded floor with the rest of our sweaty classmates.

The surface of the street could have grilled a fish, and the temperature within the auditorium would have made a baker want his job back.

Hundreds of eager faces were waiting for Peking Man to perform his annual ritual. Everyone was solemn, pressured by peers, family, and society to succeed. What was usually a rowdy crowd now sat quietly, as if awaiting sentencing.

Peking Man strolled in, sporting a T-shirt two sizes too small that revealed a couple of inches of his hairy potbelly and a pair of loose shorts that were cut too long. His legs were more bent than they appeared under long pants. That explained his unique side-to-side, rolling walk.

The crowd took a deep breath. It would be our first brush with the examinations; it brought a raw awakening within us.

Peking Man was silent and serious. He gazed at us with the look of a savior, a doctor. *I know your pain and I am here to take it away.*

His eyes sparkled with those wild lights so rare among modern men.

He opened his mouth a couple of times, but no words came out. A stutterer was a stutterer. On the third try, he made it. A loud sound filled the hall with echoes; it sounded like a cry from some ancient creature, but our hearts responded to it. It was a war cry.

"My students!" he called. "This is a battle and I am here to give you the weapons!" Any other day, the house would have rocked with laughter at so silly a declaration, but not that day. That day we believed him. It was wartime, us against the world, and it felt good to have Peking Man on our side. I felt like standing and saluting our hairy commander, the Monkey King.

"I have made my decisions after a long and hard search." He rolled his sad eyes, then refocused them on us.

"Here are my top selections for the year." He threw open a portable blackboard. Written on it were four long essay questions. The crowd scribbled furiously. There were only the sounds of pen fighting paper and the noisy breathing of Peking Man, who seemed to have a loose valve somewhere, another of his unevolved organs.

He then went on to explain the tricky points hidden in the questions, piloting us through them like a seasoned sailor in troubled waters. He dodged, turned, and twisted. His logic was clear and his delivery forceful. His face gradually wrinkled into a smile. Normally when he smiled, we ducked our heads, for no one wanted to witness the display of his big yellow teeth. But this time it was comforting, in a devious way. To us, those teeth were weapons.

"Each of these questions could be worth twenty-five percent of the score. Nail the answers in your brain. If any of you comes out of the test missing these questions, any part of them, you will not call me your teacher anymore. Now go." He leaned on his elbows and nodded his huge head, indicating his farewell to all our miserable souls. We rushed out of the hall for some fresh air. Another five minutes and some of us would have been carried out on stretchers.

The day before the tests, the street of Yellow Stone was alive with thousands of applicants coming to town to see the test site so that they wouldn't get lost in the next day's frenzy and confusion. Stone-faced militiamen walked the sealed sections of the school. The test-takers nervously looked beyond the yellow ribbon. For the well prepared, that day was the day to rest. The three long days of test-taking would be exhausting, to say the least. I saw the Head, the snob, dribbling a basketball absentmindedly, like a girl. Silently, I wished him luck: *May he open his paper and not know a thing.*

Others were just sitting around chatting, killing time. Han, my elementary school enemy, wasn't one of them. He had been studying, but the stuff was coming out from his granite head, his mom said. That day, he was sitting before a tall pile of books, not knowing which one to read.

His mom said he wouldn't eat, talk, or sleep. I also wished him luck and hoped that he'd faint on the floor of the test site and never wake up.

Since early morning, Dad's friends and neighbors had been coming by to wish us good luck. Ar Duang, whose son was Dad's patient, carried a large basket of fruit and insisted that we eat it all so that we would have fresh minds. Jin mingled with our guests in the living room, taking it easy. I knew he would do well. He was smiling and looked relaxed. I had gotten up at five and had washed my face extra carefully. Mom and I had prayed and kowtowed before every single god in her shrine. She had just unearthed a new one called the God of Wisdom and wanted me to beg hard before him. I had slammed about ten big ones to him, and I was sure every one of them would be worth something.

I was the only one from the town of Yellow Stone to register as an English major; only eight others in the commune were taking that major. So the National Examination Commission decided to lump us together and have all nine of us take the entire three-day exam in the city of Putien, where our final subject exam, English, was to be given.

Everyone in my family silently watched me pack a foldable bamboo mat, a sack of rice, my chopsticks, a rice pot, two bags of books, and some clothes. My youngest sister, Huang, was pumping air into a borrowed old bike. She would be giving me a ride to Putien. It felt as if they were sending me off to the battlefield, a place so far away that my family couldn't be with me. I felt an inner sadness, but I didn't show it. I was sixteen. I threw my luggage over my back, pushed out my chest, and smiled broadly at everyone. I wanted to tell them by my actions that I was brave and ready to take on the enemy.

Right before I stepped into the street, I turned and ran upstairs to my window. I knelt down and begged my grandfather to come with me to Putien and watch over me as I wrote the answers. He had loved me so deeply and had expected so much of me. It was he who had taught me the first strokes of calligraphy, his hands over mine. I needed him now more than ever. I told him that I would do honor to his name and that all his sufferings at the end of his life were not in vain because they had given me strength and would be the basis of all my success.

Tears filled my eyes as I called on his spirit again and again.

On the way to Putien, Huang and I talked for a while; then I took out my flash cards to review the English conjugations. I remembered them so well that I was sick of them, but I was terrified my memory might suddenly fail and all that knowledge disappear without a trace. We arrived at Hillside High School at the edge of Putien after three hours of hard pedaling against a headwind. The school had been temporarily converted into a camp for the test-takers from around the county. I followed the sign and found my name on the door of a dark classroom. I settled in and sent my sister home before sunset.

It was a zoo. At least a thousand students were bunking there for the next three days. The kitchen was overcrowded. I had put my rice pot in the steamer in the afternoon; it took me half an hour to locate it at dinnertime. I ate my cold rice with dried fish on the lawn in the playground and stared at the stars. I had intended to do some studying before going to sleep, but it was impossible. There was no light, no room, and I was constantly surrounded by a mob of mosquitoes. Like the city people, the mosquitoes here were sleazy. Their snouts drilled like needles and their sting stayed with you for a long time.

Daylight finally came. I crept to a quiet spot and knelt down for a brief prayer, then fought my way through the kitchen, this time easily finding my rice pot. The trick was to put it in late and get it out early.

I slowly swallowed half the rice I had steamed and left the other half uneaten.

The first test was Chinese. I was ready.

At seven-thirty, a man led the nine of us English majors on a milelong hike. We found our test site at the top of a hill and waited outside like runners at the starting line, ready to dash as soon as the bell rang. Rich kids arrived with their big-shot daddies in cars that left a dusty trail. City boys had long greased hair and fashionable clothes; the girls had long silky legs, partially covered by flowing skirts. I wore a yellowed cutoff shirt, a straw hat, and shorts, and was barefoot. Nobody looked my way, as if they had sized me up in a second and immediately dismissed me as an ignorant country bumpkin in the wrong crowd.

I was thirsty, dizzy, weak, and tired and felt the need to go to the bathroom again despite having visited it only five minutes before. I closed my eyes and prayed in silence as I waited in agony for the time to pass.

Grandpa, dear Grandpa, help me now.

The bell brought me back to reality. I ran into my test room, sat in my numbered seat, and closed my eyes again, holding my sealed questions. I felt like puking. My hands were trembling.

The proctor, a bespectacled bald man, nodded at me with a kind smile. "You may start now," he said.

I broke the seal with my pen. As I focused my eyes on the first question, there was a sudden rush of blood to my head. My mind went blank, and I had to grit my teeth and grip my table to let the feeling pass. No wonder some people were carried out by ambulance. I didn't want to be one of them. Slowly, the darkness receded. I read and reread the question and wrote down the first answer of the day.

The test lasted for four hours and ended with a long composition that was worth forty-five percent of the score. I came out smiling to myself. The first thing I did was head for a quiet corner to kneel and thank all the good gods who had helped me through this first test.

I saw others, strangers to each other, chatting and talking excitedly. I didn't want to get involved. It was over.

I stayed on the hilltop under a tall tree, munched on some dried fish, drank some water, and reviewed my history flash cards. There was a guard sitting near me. I gave him a Flying Horse and asked him to wake me if he found me dozing off and to make sure I wasn't late for the test.

At ten minutes to two, I put away my history book and looked for signs of the guard. He was snoring away like a buffalo, his lips twitching. Obviously he was having an erotic dream of some sort. Too many young females taking the test were wearing enticing skirts.

I smiled from ear to ear when I opened my history paper. Peking Man had guessed two of the four questions. Each would bring me fifteen percent of the total score. I let out an animal cry of ecstasy as I left the room, then danced down the stairs. Others watched as though I were crazy. Long live

Peking Man! I knew all the answers and had had plenty of time to check every nuance of the questions, as Peking Man had taught us to do, analytically and clearly. I wanted to take a picture of him and frame it above my college bunk bed and pray to him. He was almost a god. They should at least make him a local god of Yellow Stone High and give him whatever he wanted from life.

That evening I ate twice as much as the day before. I was halfway through—only three more subjects to go.

I sailed through the second day like a sleek sailboat.

The English test came last, and it came as no surprise. I knew every word and irregular conjugation. There was a long translated article, a story about a magic ring. I had never felt as confident in an examination before. The large bag of exercises given to me by Professor Wei covered all the questions and more. I wanted to hug her and tell her she should become a goddess too, and that I would frame her picture and worship it every day.

When I walked out of the test room for the last time, my burden dropped to the ground. I was free.

Even the city folks began to look okay to me. I was ready to hug and embrace anyone when I saw my brother looking for me. I ran over to him and we shook hands frantically.

"How did you do?" he asked.

"Couldn't have done better," I said, out of breath.

He had come to pick me up and share all the details of the experience we had come through together. We forgot about our fatigue and talked, laughed, smoked, and talked some more. We compared answers, thinking that we had gotten about eighty-five percent right. We were ecstatic.

We rode home in the fading sunlight. The breeze was

gentle, the air cool. Our hearts were light. My brother had become my best friend. We had fought together and at least in our hearts we knew that we had won.

The next day I woke up to the painful twisting of my ears and nose.

I tried to get up but my legs were pinned down. I opened my eyes to see my four friends, making ugly faces as they tried to wake me up.

"Hey, what's up?" I rubbed my eyes.

"We're taking you hunting, college man," Siang said. "I heard you did well in the tests."

"Yeah, everyone's talking about it." Mo Gong gave my ear another twist.

"We're gonna take you out for a day of fun." Yi pulled my quilt off and lay beside me.

Sen was nudging my behind with the butt of his hunting rifle.

"Wake up. We've got catching up to do. Who knows, you're probably gonna be outta here in no time."

I spent the whole day shooting birds in the thick woods, eating fruit, and smoking. Sen had brought a bottle of liquor, which we passed around. Mo Gong was a little woozy after a few greedy gulps. We sent him to pick up the fallen birds. At one point, he stumbled into wet mud and almost sank into a mudhole. We had to pull him out. Then he rolled on the ground until dried leaves stuck all over his body, and started dancing around like an aborigine, singing weird tunes that sounded like Japanese folk songs. I threw more leaves on him and he danced even more madly. Sen passed the bottle to him and he finished it off. Totally drunk, he started to laugh so heartily that it began to sound like crying. Then he collapsed on the floor, still in a fit of uncontrollable laughter. We had to kick him to stop his craziness. Then we carried him to the middle of a wooden bridge and dropped him into the Dong Jing River. He continued laughing until he sank beneath the water.

We applauded, expecting to see him jump up like a fish for air. But one minute passed, then two. We looked at each other.

"Don't worry. He's fooling us this time." Sen was calm.

"He could never hold his breath for that long," I said.

"He's a better swimmer than you are."

"But he could be dead. He's drunk, remember."

"Even a drunk is always thirty percent clearheaded. Don't let him fool you," Yi said.

"The guy is dying! Do something! I'm going down there." I took off my shirt and jumped into the water. My actions brought them all to the edge.

Suddenly, Mo Gong shot up like a fish and let out a wild cry. "I got you!"

"See, I told you," Sen said.

Mo Gong swam to the edge. "I saw it all. Da was the most worried about me. Not you guys. If I'd come up and seen you still there on the bridge, smiling, I woulda quit being your friends. I really liked that, Da. Your shorts are soaked." We splashed water all over him and forced him into the river again.

Jin's mood waxed and waned in a daily cycle. Some days he thought he had scored well, other days he thought he had drilled holes in the boat and was sinking. For the moment, he threw himself into farmwork. On a good day, he would hum and whistle, digging the field in readiness for the autumn bean season. He was the amicable old Jin everyone liked. On a bad day, he would stay in bed really late, the quilt over his head, thinking of all the questions he had missed. He used the abacus in his head and crunched the total score of his tests. But the more he crunched, the lower his scores got. He made himself miserable. We called it the Cousin Tan factor.

In the evening, I sat with him in our backyard and chatted. Mom and Dad had given me the job of encouraging him. They didn't want to see him turn into a nut. I would pull out our bamboo abacus and play with my estimate of his scores as he remembered them. When he said seventy percent, I threw in a modest five percent markup. In the end, the total looked fine. He was surprised by my estimate and wondered how I had come up with it. I told him he was too hard on himself; then I'd go to our kitchen and pour some locally brewed liquor for him. Resistant at first, he would drink it nonetheless. It would loosen him up, and we and the rest of the family would sit talking in the moonlight, late into the night.

I was the opposite. My own estimate of my scores kept going up.

Everyone in the family laughed at me. It was a pure gut feeling, but they believed me and were glad for me. No one stopped me from climbing my ladder of dreams.

A month later, rumors began to circulate that the papers had all been graded and the scores were in. The scores were low across the board. All the test-takers gossiped among themselves. Jin at this point didn't care anymore. It only made me pray harder each night, hitting my head against the soft pillows in obeisance to all the gods I assembled in my head, to whom I read off my list of wishes. The list got longer each day and the list of promises to the gods grew more generous. I went from one little piglet for each god to five piglets and two cows as sacrifices if all the items on my list came true. And I knew that if that happened I would probably have to bankrupt our family, returning all our worldly possessions to the places they had come from. But that didn't stop me. I figured we could always deliver the sacrifices gradually, or even make out an IOU for the gods. When all was repaid, we would add on a handsome interest. They would have no problem with that.

During the course of the morning, word leaked out about the score line. This was a line the government drew to cut off the successful applicants from the unsuccessful ones. It was based on how many slots were open for college enrollment that year: if there were only 100 openings, the cutoff line would be set after the top one 100 scores. Everyone above that line was guaranteed a place in college, while the rest of the applicants wouldn't be considered at all. This year's cutoff point was 300 out of the total 500 points possible.

The news sent chills down our spines. We all must have done terribly.

Just after midnight, the messenger, Chung, ran into our house, sweat covering his red face. He was breathless from the three-hour ride that he had just cut to two. We surrounded him, watching his heaving chest with great anxiety.

"Water," he croaked.

"The scores first," Dad said.

"I'm really thirsty."

"The scores." Dad's voice had never been that loud with a friend before.

Chung smiled.

We stood by, our hearts in our throats.

"Jin first." Chung swallowed. "Three hundred and fifty." There was an odd lull. Jin was in. His face first turned ashen, then red. He was speechless.

"How about Da?"

"You want to know?"

"Yes, yes. What is it?"

"Three hundred and eighty!" I felt the blood shoot up to the very top of my head. All the muscles in my arms twitched uncontrollably.

"I'm not finished yet. According to the record, Da has one of the highest liberal arts scores in the province of Fujian, including the big cities of Fuzhou, Amoy, Chuangzhou, and Nanping—out of hundreds of thousands of test-takers." There were no joyful shouts or happy dances, only tears. It was a moment of triumph and happiness for the whole Chen family. Mom was in Dad's arms; my sisters were sniffling and holding each other. Jin and I shook hands wildly.

A dirt-poor country boy, beating all the city brats. I couldn't believe it. It was about forty points higher than my highest estimate. I could kowtow forever.

TWENTY-FOUR

Mom asked me to walk to her brother's house to tell Cousin Tan the news. I took the narrow road through the green fields. The fresh sea wind made the young rice dance and woke up my dizzy mind, still dazed with the intoxicating news.

Cousin Tan was holding court at his house with a few of his classmates from AU. I heard carefree laughter as I entered. They were having tea. I wanted to drop the bomb and have the AU boys running for cover. Tan stood up as I came through the door. Smart guy, he sensed something.

"Did you hear anything?" he asked.

I stood there, trying to catch my breath.

"Is it bad news?" he asked anxiously.

I shook my head. I didn't want to seem too eager to impress a bunch of AU guys, all of whom were proudly wearing their white-and-red school badges.

"Jin got three hundred and fifty," I said.

"Well, that's very high." Tan knitted his intellectual brows together with disbelief. "How about you?"

I took another deep breath.

"You didn't make it?" He started to smile and stretch out his uncallused hands to press on me his subtle condolence. I knew that look.

"My score was three hundred and eighty." All his cronies stood up.

"What did you say?" Tan didn't believe his ears.

"Three hundred and eighty," I repeated.

Silence.

"You've got to be kidding," Tan said absentmindedly, making a readjustment in his mind. "I'm sure AU would consider you for their famous English department."

"Give me a break, Tan," one of his classmates said. "This fellow doesn't want to go to a college isolated on a little island in the corner of China. It's okay for a bunch of older guys to study finance there, but for English, he should and *could* go to big cities like Beijing or Shanghai."

"I'll think about all the options," I said diplomatically. "I'm sure AU would be an excellent choice also." I didn't want to hurt Tan's pride.

After all, I still loved and respected my cousin. He had paved the road for Jin and me and had given us hope when we were just another landlord's family, waiting to be wasted by Communism.

I said good-bye to them and told them I wanted to go take a long nap.

They laughed and saw me to the door, slapping my shoulder in congratulation. Cousin Tan affectionately pinched the back of my neck.

Coming from a bunch of college men, I considered that

the red–carpet treatment. I was one of the boys now. In a single moment, I had arrived.

I took the same route back home to avoid being stared at in the street. By now, Yellow Stone would be like dry hay aflame with the breaking news about the Chen brothers. Having one child in a family going to college was an eye-opener, but two at the same time? The town wouldn't be able to sleep for a long while. The shock would be reverberating through the people by now.

Some people in Yellow Stone wouldn't be able to take such an insulting assault on their turf. Two landlord's children, hitting the jackpot at the same time? No way. There would be hostile letters of protest, ghostwritten and sent anonymously to the Board of Education, filled with big fat lies, aiming to try to stop us. There would be people gritting their teeth at this very moment, swearing to poke a hole in our balloon and let our dream be just another dream. I knew it was coming and that we should appear modest and undeserving in public.

Mom shut the front door early and prepared a simple dinner. We moved our dining table to the backyard. Everyone was whispering as we set the table and prepared the food. My sisters had left work early.

The young rice plants could wait, but the celebration could not.

We sat close together around the round table, all seven of us. It was a little crowded, and we kicked each other under the table and fought with our chopsticks for the last bite as we had when we were children.

We whispered and laughed quietly, lest there were ears listening outside the walls. It was okay to let people know when you were suffering, but not when you were celebrating. They turned jealous, and evil things were bred from the seeds of jealousy.

Dad smiled like a carefree lion, smoking his pipe, while my mom still sniffled over the shock of the news. It had shaken her up in a very pleasant way. They both confessed that it was the best day of their lives. They were so happy and proud. It made their decades of suffering worthwhile. Our sisters poked us with challenging questions, like which pretty girls we would consider as brides. We went through a list with mock interest: none of them seemed perfect. The appealing ones didn't have the cows necessary for a dowry, while the ugly ones had plenty.

Our sisters giggled and giggled over our silly discussion.

We dreamed and sat there, just staring at a perfect Yellow Stone sunset.

We were given an application form to fill out, along with a list of slots open to Fujian students at all the colleges. The slots for English majors were pathetically few. From the top down, there was only one at Beijing First Foreign Language Institute and two at Beijing Second Foreign Language Institute. There was one opening at Shanghai Foreign Language Institute, a few more at other cities like Nanjing and Fuzhou, and twenty at Amoy University. There were other tempting slots in foreign trade and international journalism, both of which required a strong English performance.

The school counselor advised me that my score put me in the top two percent of all applicants. Any college I picked could be mine. My brother's score also qualified him for a leading university. He had his mind set on finance, and his university choices were all near home. He wanted to be close to the family. But they fully supported my choice, Beijing First Foreign Language Institute, the top spot on that year's roster. I was the bird that had to fly far and high, and they wanted me to reach for the sky because I thought I could. And now they, too, were beginning to think that I could.

I turned in my application at the commune headquarters, an office near the commune jail in which the principal of my elementary school had once wanted to put me.

The lady clerk smiled at me when she saw my name and choice.

"You're the star they have been talking about. I have heard your story. I want my son to do just as well as you did. Would you mind meeting him?" she asked.

"Sure." She stood up, went to the back room, and brought out a two-year-old toddler.

"Shake hands with him, son." She grabbed her son's chubby, sticky hand, and I shook it. The kid was a little shy. I pinched his rosy cheek.

"Thank you. I hope he remembers meeting you." I felt flattered. Overnight, I had become the model son to all moms.

As I headed out, she stopped me. "Here, I've got something for you. Take these and burn them." There were a dozen badly written, lying letters of protest against Jin and me.

I ran behind the headquarters building and found a seat beneath a tree. I went through all the letters quickly. The most ridiculous accusation was a claim that Jin and I had cheated by swapping answers in the public toilets during the exam. *Yeah, right.* Jin and I had taken the tests forty miles apart. Others claimed we were from a landlord's family and didn't deserve to be in college—old clichés and other garbage. One letter said that my brother had poor eyesight and that I hung out with bad company. That was true, but did it matter?

Two days later, we got a notice from the county that said we had to have a complete physical examination. I didn't eat or sleep too well that night. Maybe my eyes would be too weak or my legs too short. I had no muscles and was all bones. My belly button was too deep, my nipples too far apart, and my ribs heaved like an accordion. Why would our country want to invest four years of college in such a shaky person?

We went on the commune's muddy tractor. There were no showy flowers pinned on our chests or anything like that. We arrived at Putien County Hospital a little late because we had had to fill the gas tank, and the driver had stopped to push a fallen tree to the side of the narrow road, then had brawled for a good ten minutes with the farmer who owned the tree.

The nurse rushed us through a minor check, then asked us to take off all our clothes.

"Our clothes?"

"Yeah, now." My brother and I squirmed uncomfortably. We finally stood there in our underwear, the last shred of our male dignity hanging loose.

"What's the matter? Come on, drop it, I don't have all day. There's a hundred female applicants waiting for me." That sent us flying. We faced the wall and dropped our protection.

We stared at each other with goose bumps crawling over our bodies like ants. It was the first time we had seen each other naked. The nurse's cold hands ran over a few things. Then she took off her plastic gloves with a disgusted look, tossed them into a garbage can, and washed her hands.

We had passed.

"I guess nothing's missing," Jin said, pulling up his shorts.

"I guess so. Mom and Dad made us right and whole." We laughed and were out of the exam room in a second.

Not surprisingly, Jin got some generous proposals of marriage from the beauties of Yellow Stone and beyond. There were nurses, teachers, salesclerks, secretaries, and actresses. Jin showed no interest. He wanted to consider marriage only after college. But Mom, Dad, and our sisters were having a terrific time going through the list, studying them as if for real. They even broke into serious arguments over the merits of their personal choices. Some of the girls on the list shied away whenever they passed our house, acutely aware that they were being scrutinized.

One night a pretty little girl no more than seven or eight ran to our house and said that her dad was inviting me to her house to watch television. There was a special program on that night. The invitation came out of the blue. The girl turned out to be the youngest daughter of the party secretary of our commune. He was the only person in Yellow Stone to have a TV, a nine-inch black-and-white one, which he proudly placed on top of a table in the front yard. In the evenings, he would invite the town's small group of dignitaries to watch the nightly programs, starting at seven and ending at eleven. Receiving an invitation from him to witness the magic of his nine-incher was like being given his personal seal of approval. The next day the whole town would know who was there and why.

Mom was obviously flattered by the invitation and asked

me to take a long bath and put on my best white shirt and a new pair of sandals. I had dinner early, then strolled over the bridge to his walled estate. There were about fifty people sitting, standing, and squatting outside the gate.

They were there in the hope that the party secretary might be in a generous mood and let them in. If not, they would be perfectly content sitting outside the wall all night long, listening to the TV as though it were a radio.

The crowd parted as I strolled through the throng. The party secretary stood at the door, fanning away flies with a dried coconut leaf. His potbelly was barely covered by his shorts. He welcomed me enthusiastically.

"There is a drama at nine tonight that I thought you might want to see," he said.

"Thank you for the invitation. I love drama."

"I thought you would." I entered the door; inside was another world. There were flowers in pots, a tea table, and lush sofas scattered around a stand where the TV proudly sat, precious modern magic. It was the first time I had ever seen a television.

The party secretary showed me to a prominent seat as all present stood up to meet me. I bowed to them like a spineless sucker. The party vice secretary, the head of the commune's women's group, the head of the Young Leaguers, and a few good-looking ladies were there. I was embarrassed by the attention. These guys had hung my dad up by his thumbs a few years ago, had locked my sister up for selling our clothing ration coupons, had shortened my grandfather's life and made his last days in this world a living hell. Now they all smiled and shook hands with me, praising me for the high scores. It felt strange, but extraordinarily good.

I sat down. A pretty girl, the eldest daughter of the host,

carried over a cup of steaming tea on an elegant tray and served me with a sweet smile. I took the tea with a humble heart, outwardly trying to be nonchalant. She sat beside me and explained the high technology of the nine-inch black box. I felt uneasy chatting with her. It was a challenge to conduct a civil conversation without spilling my tea.

The TV blinked all night, the reception was spotty, and when thick clouds passed overhead, blurring it even more, the audience had to guess at what was happening on the screen. It was a milestone in my book, nonetheless. The daughter kept pouring me tea, and I kept running to their bathroom. I left with the rest of the crowd when the TV screen turned white with busy little dots. At home, Mom had waited up to question me about how I had been received. She wanted all the details.

I gave her a full and complete report, and she smiled with satisfaction.

TWENTY-FIVE

造

I went to the post office every morning and sorted the mail with the clerk. This chubby lady was a one-woman show: she was the phone operator, mail deliverer, telegram person, and counter clerk, who sold stamps and sealed packages. She was also the mother of the two kids who played on the dirt floor and watched the door for her. Whenever the truck arrived, the eldest kid would shout that the mail was in from Putien. His mom would come out, and I would help her carry it in. When she was out on her bike delivering the mail, her mother-in-law took over watching the children and the switchboard. No matter how shabby, the post office was a crucial message center: it held my hopes and dreams.

I sat on the doorstep, played with the kids, and looked for the green post office truck from Putien each morning. Whenever it came, my heart would race and my head would begin to throb with anticipation.

One fine autumn day, the kid yelled as usual, and his mom

and I carried in an unusually large load. She threw me the stack of mail, the sorting of which had become my routine, and I clawed through it carefully and quickly.

A large registered envelope dropped out of the stack. The return address looked familiar.

Beijing First Foreign Language Institute.

It was addressed to Comrade Chen Da.

I jumped up and screamed at the clerk. She handed me a pair of scissors and I slit open the envelope.

In one simple sentence, the letter informed me that I had been admitted into Beijing Language Institute's English department, and that I was expected to report on campus within a month.

I ran home as fast as I could.

Mom, Dad, and the whole family were on hand to congratulate me.

We studied the letter and the information they had sent about the department and the college. The picture of the college was a treasure.

My dream had come true. I would be off to Beijing to study English.

I would be the first one in the history of Yellow Stone High to do so.

Now I had a future, a bright one. In a few years, I would be fluent in English, could go to work for the Foreign Ministry and would converse in that fine language with fine people in an elegant international setting. Other things would follow, and I would be able to take care of my wonderful family and give them all that had been denied them.

Though I had never set foot outside my county and Putien was the largest city I had ever been to, my mind had wings, and it had traveled far away.

I made a list of people to visit before I left. Professor Wei was at the top. She had been away traveling with her sister since I took the test, but now she was back.

I took two ducks and visited her one afternoon. She opened the door and made me tell her what had happened. I said we should talk inside. She said she couldn't wait another second.

Beijing First Foreign Language Institute, I said.

She said she couldn't believe it.

She jumped up and down like a small child and said she was so glad, she wanted to hug me and thank me for being such a good student.

We hugged and she rested her head on my shoulder. I felt her tears on my white shirt. She was having a good time.

I promised to write and report all my progress to her. She looked at me and shook her head slowly, still incredulous. Her hands cupped her delicate face as she stood in her doorway waiting until I disappeared into the woods.

Of course, her mean dog was still angry at me. He seemed to be saying, *I'm the only one in town to see through you. You are nothing but a country boy and will always be a country boy.* I made peace with myself and agreed with the dog for the first time. I would always be a country boy, no more, no less.

Dad gave me another list of people to visit, the older generation, his friends and those relatives with whom we had lost contact during the tough times. I visited them all and was received warmly and with respect.

My four buddies reappeared from nowhere one day and had two bikes on hand. They took me to a fancy restaurant in Putien, one that we used to look at from a distance as we smelled the fine aromas wafting from the ventilation window, trying to guess the price of each smell.

We boasted and talked about the old days. Mo Gong took off his old leather shoes and said I would need them in a cold city like Beijing. We went to a photo studio and froze our memory into a black-and-white picture.

Meanwhile, at home we were getting worried about Jin's admission. He was a little older than the usual college student, and we suspected that someone might have been making trouble for him. With his score, he should have received letters from the colleges by now. The whole family was caught between us two. I was in the celebrating mood, while he still waited in agony. There had been cases where applicants with high scores had been left out by clerical error. He began to go to the post office just as I had, waiting every day. He, too, played with the kids and helped the lady clerk with her routine.

Finally, two days before I was about to leave, his letter came.

It was a moment of great happiness for all of us. Mom and Dad, who were hardened by many years of suffering and deprivation, rarely revealed their emotions, but now I saw Dad collapse into a chair, bury his face in his shaking hands, and weep. Mom sat down also and let loose a torrent. Everyone was sniffling.

Thirty years of humiliation had suddenly come to an end. Two sons had been accepted into leading universities within the same year. Mom and Dad had never dreamed of such a day. They had thought we were finished. Kicked around in school, I had almost dropped out many times. Jin had been forced to quit school at the age of twelve to become a farmer with nothing to look forward to but blisters on his tender hands, being spat upon by the older farmers, and doing backbreaking work that had taken away ten prime years of his life. There had been years of no hope, no dreams, only tears, hunger, shame, and darkness.

I held my brother's shoulders as he sobbed. But it was soon over. He was the first to wipe his eyes and smile broadly at everyone. All the tears were ended.

During the next two days, Jin threw himself into packing for me as I went around bowing and thanking everyone in the neighborhood.

My heart was full of gratitude to even the meanest people on the street who used to slight us. I bade good-bye to them all. They were touched and shook my hand firmly. They said they would try to take care of my parents while Jin and I were gone. I thanked them again.

On the day of my departure, we got up early. Mom prepared all the cows and pigs I had promised the gods and Buddha. She made them with flour and water and painted them red. I kowtowed a thousand times and thanked the gods for making my dream come true.

Mom gave me an embroidered silk bag filled with dust from the incense holder and a pinch of soil from Yellow Stone. She asked me to carry it with me to Beijing and to spread it on the ground there when I arrived. It would ensure protection from the gods and Buddha at home. I hid the bag safely in the middle of my wooden trunk.

After breakfast, I checked my train ticket for the last time. Dad, my sisters, and Jin had borrowed bikes and were coming to Putien to see me off at the bus station. I hugged Mom at the door again and again.

She cried, but a smile shone through her tears. She pulled me once more into her arms, then gently pushed me away and nodded. Only at that moment, as I looked at her, did I realize that she was the most beautiful woman in the whole world and that I was going to miss her when I was thousands of miles away in Beijing.

As I hopped up onto the backseat of one of the bikes, our neighbors came out to wave good-bye to me. The cigarette man, Liang, was old now. He wobbled to the edge and smiled and bowed to me. The doctor was also there, waving his cane in my direction. Some neighbors stood at my mom's side, comforting her. I took a long last look at the cobbled street of Yellow Stone, the Dong Jing River, and the Ching Mountain, looming tall in the background.

Good-bye, Yellow Stone. I am forever your son.

We rode on our four bikes, chatting and laughing on the way to the bus station. I had never seen Dad so happy and carefree. He joked and told stories about my childhood. We arrived at noon. My bus was already boarding.

Jin was coming with me to Fuzhou to see me off at the train station, because I had never seen a train before. Without his guidance, it would be Da in Wonderland, running after the train as it left. I had never been on a bus before, either. The only motor vehicle I had ridden on was the commune's noisy tractor.

Together Jin and I threw my heavy wooden trunk onto the overloaded luggage rack on top of the shaky, dusty bus. Then we squeezed into a crowded seat that was marked for four people but actually had six occupying it. My sisters came onto the bus and hugged me tearfully; then Dad climbed up the steps. He stumbled, and I sprang out of my seat to meet him. He gave me a bear hug. I was surrounded once more by the same warmth I used to feel as a small kid hiding under his padded cotton overcoat. He took my face in his hands and bit his lower lip until it turned pale.

"I want to get some fruit for you, son. You wait." He

stumbled down from the bus and ran toward a fruit stand a few yards away. His back was hunched over, and his steps were slower than he wanted them to be. He climbed over the guardrail that separated the passengers from the onlookers and almost fell.

When he came back, the engine had already started. Dad walked in front of the bus to stop it. The driver was yelling at him. He ran to the window where we sat and passed four pears to me. He was out of breath and looked very tired. His eyes were wet, but there was a smile on his wrinkled face. I couldn't help the tears that rolled down my cheeks as we pulled away from the crowded station. Dad stood there waving to me. I craned my neck until I could see him no longer.

I love you, Dad. I am your son forever.

AFTERWORD

After graduating from college, my brother became general manager of the biggest paper factory in Fujiang province. It is a dream come true. To this day, he still gets teary talking about life during the Cultural Revolution as compared to his life now. He is happily married to his wonderful college-educated engineer wife, which is another achievement in itself—for had the Cultural Revolution continued, he would probably have ended up an unwilling monk.

My three sisters have all married happily as well. Si is now the owner of a small store, Huang a jewelry trader, and Ke a musician.

I broke all the ropes that were meant to tie me down, succeeded as a college student, and then went on to receive a full scholarship to attend Columbia University Law School in New York. Not long after, I fell in love with and married a beautiful Chinese medical student. We now live happily with our two young children in the Hudson Valley, where I'll continue to tell my tales of hope in the land called China.

ABOUT THE AUTHOR

Da Chen is a graduate of Columbia University Law School. A brush calligrapher of great spirituality who also plays the classical bamboo flute, he lives in New York's Hudson Valley with his wife and two small children.